WRITING SCIENCE FICTION, FANTASY & HORROR

GW00671455

How To Books on Successful Writing

Copyright & Law for Writers
Creating a Twist in the Tale
Creative Writing
How to Be a Freelance Journalist
How to Publish a Book
How to Publish a Newsletter
How to Start Word Processing
How to Write a Press Release
How to Write a Report
How to Write an Assignment
How to Write an Essay
How to Write & Sell Computer Software
How to Write Business Letters
How to Write for Publication
How to Write for Television
How to Write Your Dissertation
Mastering Business English
Starting to Write
Writing a Nonfiction Book
Writing & Selling a Novel
Writing Reviews
Writing Romantic Fiction
Writing Science Fiction, Fantasy & Horror

Other titles in preparation

The How To series now contains more than 200 titles in the
following categories:

Business Basics
Family Reference
Jobs & Careers
Living & Working Abroad
Student Handbooks
Successful Writing

Please send for a free copy of the latest catalogue for full details
(see back cover for address).

WRITING SCIENCE FICTION FANTASY & HORROR

How to create successful work
for publication

Christopher Kenworthy

WHAT MAKES YOU THINK
YOU'D BE GOOD AT
WRITING SCIENCE FICTION?

How To Books

Cartoons by Mike Flanagan

British Library Cataloguing-in-Publication data
A catalogue record for this book is available from the British Library.

© Copyright 1997 by Christopher Kenworthy.

First published in 1997 by How To Books Ltd, 3 Newtec Place,
Magdalen Road, Oxford OX4 1RE, United Kingdom.
Tel: (01865) 793806. Fax: (01865) 248780.

Note: The material contained in this book is set out in good faith for
general guidance and no liability can be accepted for loss or expense
incurred as a result of relying in particular circumstances on statements
made in the book. The laws and regulations are complex and liable to
change, and readers should check the current position with the relevant
authorities before making personal arrangements.

Produced for How To Books by Deer Park Productions.
Typeset by Kestrel Data, Exeter.
Printed and bound in Great Britain by
Cromwell Press, Broughton Gifford, Melksham, Wiltshire.

Contents

5

List of Illustrations

Preface

What would happen if the government was working in secret with an alien race? How would we cope with interstellar travel? What will happen when we colonise Mars? What will we do if machines become conscious?

The answers are found in science fiction. These questions have been answered many times, in different ways, by thousands of writers. If you want to be a science fiction writer you will find new questions, and you will answer them in an original way.

As a science fiction writer you will move readers with an astounding sense of wonder, while revealing the precise detail of human existence. Science fiction is a unique form of literature, because you are free to explore any possible future that comes to mind. Whatever wonders you imagine, whatever fears darken your thoughts, you are free to express them through science fiction.

Science fiction, fantasy and horror are the only forms of writing where you create whole worlds. While inventing characters and locations to tell your story, you will also create new civilisations, planets and technologies. This is why science fiction is demanding of creativity, but also why it is so rewarding.

No book can turn you into a writer, but it can guide your work if you are prepared to put in the effort. This book suggests methods of working that will help you to find ideas, characters and themes, so that you can create believable stories. You will avoid the basic pitfalls that plague most writers, while developing an approach to writing that suits you best. With creative effort, and persistence, *you* can learn to write science fiction, fantasy and horror stories.

Christopher Kenworthy

Is This You?

Librarian

First time writer

Part-time writer

Freelance writer

Short story writer

Novelist

Creative thinker

Science fiction reader

Horror reader

Fantasy reader

General reader

Science fiction cinema fan

Star Trek fan

X-Files fan

'Cult TV' fan

Creative writing student

English student

English teacher

Academic

Publisher

Editor

Reviewer

1
Getting Started

If you want to be a science fiction writer, this book will teach you everything you need to know. It will show you how to create new worlds and characters, developing original ideas into stories that sell.

Science fiction has never been more popular. From TV series such as *Star Trek Voyager, Highlander* and the *X-files*, through to the novels of Iain Banks and Kim Stanley Robinson, science fiction can earn big money.

Unlike other forms of fiction, science fiction looks at how the world might be when things are different. If something fundamental changes, what will become of us? What if we discover alien life? What if we learn to be immortal, or to travel to the stars? By asking such questions, and offering possible answers, science fiction reminds us of what it is to be human today.

Science fiction, fantasy and horror are published as separate genres, but they tend to overlap. By learning about the three genres together you will be able to write, rich, popular and saleable stories.

WORKING AT BEING A WRITER

To get the most from this book you must *work* at being a writer. Sculptors, musicians and painters practise their craft for many hours. Writers try to be perfect first time, but this rarely works. Practise writing, and keep working over the ideas and techniques described here.

Science fiction is more speculative, imaginative and inventive than any other type of fiction, so you will eventually adapt the techniques described to suit your own style. To begin with follow the suggestions closely, until you are able to write stories with confidence.

The discussion points at the end of each chapter are useful writing exercises. Practise writing regularly and your fiction will improve each day. It only takes a few weeks of persistence to get used to writing, if you keep at it.

WRITING SCIENCE FICTION

If you are more familiar with television and film science fiction, try reading SF stories and novels. Film and television science fiction is generally about ten years behind written SF, in terms of ideas, so you need more up-to-date knowledge. Absorb books from the recommended reading list, and subscribe to magazines such as *Interzone* and *The Third Alternative*. In a short while you will be able to submit finished stories to them, and perhaps begin working on a novel.

These days editors are looking for originality, as much as for style and technique. If you can create an original science fiction story, it will sell. Everybody is original, if they decide not to copy. Although you are free to love *Lord of the Rings, Hellraiser* and *Star Wars*, make sure that you tell your own story.

Understanding the basics

> Science fiction is about change, and always contains something that doesn't presently exist.

Science fiction has covered subjects such as:
- nano-technology
- alien contact
- time travel
- virtual reality
- artificial intelligence

and others. Although these ideas can be reworked to some extent, you will have to find original versions of the future to excite your readers.

Science fiction can deal with small ideas, such as a new type of telephone, through to the massive implications of instant interstellar travel. It can cover a few hours of existence, or a trillion-year future history. SF can be set in the near future, an alternate present, or thousands of years hence.

Dealing with emotions
Whatever the scale or timing of your stories, it is the *people* who inhabit your fiction that will interest readers. Even when writing about **aliens** and computers, the emotions should be recognisable.

The films *ET* and *Close Encounters of the Third Kind* weren't about aliens so much as the people who needed to make contact with them. *Close Encounters of the Third Kind* is about belief and responsibility, while *ET* is about adolescence and friendship. Although the SF elements are vital, these stories work because of the emotional content.

> SF stories work best when they enhance our understanding of present life.

Red Mars, by Kim Stanley Robinson, shows humans battling with ethical, engineering and social problems. The ideas and images generate a sense of wonder and spectacle, while reflecting present day life on Earth. This is the power of SF: to examine who we are, and where we are going.

Building new worlds

Every time you write an SF story you have to create an entire world. Every idea has a knock-on effect. If, for instance, we were able to develop a system of teleportation, this affects more than tourism. The whole economy could be broken down, countries might cease to exist, the use of weapons could be advanced or negated. Every idea has thousands of effects, and you must consider the impact of your technology.

Once you have found a core idea, you should try to establish how it might affect:

- the general level of technology
- political systems
- modes of transport
- employment
- sources of food
- ethnic and social groups
- relationships
- religion
- the landscape and visible environment

- housing
- entertainment.

Determine whether the technology is owned by an individual, corporation, world government, or whether it is available to all. Are its effects desirable or avoidable?

Working on details

You will need to know how the imagined world operates, to create a sense of realism. If, for example, you are writing about London two centuries from now you will have to consider which buildings are there, and why. Would the people walk, or teleport, or travel on moving platforms? Would there be office blocks, cinemas, cafés? What would people be eating and drinking? What would the conversation be about?

In all SF some things stay the same, while other things change.

Before you write a word you must gain a general impression of how your new idea, technology or political system affects the whole culture. If you are writing about a future where human labour has been almost entirely replaced by machines, would people be happy or bored? How would lifestyle, relationships and human endeavour be affected? With all that time and potential, what would humans do?

Without taking these consideration on, you will make mistakes. Readers who enjoy SF love seeing how one idea can affect a whole society.

Constructing your SF world

Building new worlds can happen in an instant, with one idea dictating all the others, or it can take many hours of note-taking, research and preparation. Remember, you are telling a story rather than journalising a possible future, but try to be as consistent and logical as possible.

World-building is also a *creative* process. By answering the questions and dealing with the implications of your idea you will find that your characters and themes become much easier to handle.

EXPLORING FANTASY

Fantasy is one of the broadest terms in all literature, because it covers a massive range of fiction.

Straight fantasy is also called **sword and sorcery** fiction, because it deals with elves, wizards, magical kingdoms, heroic quests, and the battle between good and evil. Most of these stories are written as novel trilogies, perhaps because the first major fantasy novel, J. R. R. Tolkein's *Lord of the Rings*, set this trend.

Some writers and reviewers dismiss fantasy, because it lacks the scientific reasoning of straightforward science fiction. This is unfair.

> Good fantasy is as logical and complete as the best science fiction. The difference is that the ideas and laws of the invented universe are completely imaginary, rather than derived from science.

The criticism of fantasy perhaps arises from poorly written fantasy, in which problems are solved by a new spell, or the discovery of an enchanted sword, rather than character action. This type of fiction is not satisfying, because the characters are never tested or forced to develop.

Making rules for your imagined world
To avoid this problem of character development, treat the magic elements of your imagined world as set laws. Although magic offers power, it should also have side effects and limitations. These restrictions put your characters into situations that require genuine action on their part to solve problems.

If you want to write sword and sorcery fantasy the techniques and suggestions given for science fiction also apply. Although fantasy ideas aren't based on scientific theories, they are logical and require accurate world-building.

Discovering deeper fantasy
Fantasy also refers to a type of fiction which is close to the mainstream. This is sometimes known as **magic realism, heightened realism,** or **slipstream**. These are broad terms which refer to fiction which is concerned with states of mind, rather than scientific ideas or imaginary worlds.

This type of fantasy deals with dreams, psychoactive drugs, illusions and sometimes magic. It is usually set in the modern world, with the fantastic elements blending in with ordinary life. The television series *Twin Peaks* was a perfect example of this, where the conventions of a detective series were married with a fantastic, magical background. At first, many viewers thought they were watching a straightforward mystery, but it soon became clear that strange powers were involved.

The technique also works in prose fiction, as with Trevor Hoyle's *Blind Needle* and Nicholas Royle's *Counterparts*. The merging of dreams, visions and imagined events creates a startling effect.

This type of fiction is one of the most exciting, because the magic occurs in a world that is recognisable to the reader. The magic and fantasy seem extremely realistic, because they occur in ordinary surroundings.

Incorporating reality with emotion

This type of fantasy, where the ordinary world is slightly altered, often looks at the way emotions affect reality, and vice versa. The events may be illogical at times, dictated by a character's beliefs and fears, rather than an absolute reality. If, for example, a character finds that every time he dreams about his sister a glass pearl is released from his ear, there needn't be a scientific explanation. Readers will accept that this is either symbolic or an illusion.

This freedom from science can lead to chaos, so use altered states of reality carefully. All the strange events should happen for a reason. The peculiar states of mind and the reality found in fantasy should reflect the idea or theme of your story, and the nature of your characters.

USING HORROR

Horror fiction is all about getting below the surface of things. The easy way is to split the skin and let loose a stream of blood and gristle. Although this may be dubiously entertaining, it is shallow and brief. The best way for horror writing to affect us is to get under the surface of a personality. When this is successul it can reach a depth of insight unmatched by any other type of writing.

In the best horror fiction the images and events are frightening, as well as enlightening.

The horror field is an excellent place to learn writing skills, to face up to your own emotions and generate truly moving stories. It could be said that all fiction aims to deal with truth, but horror is the fiction of total honesty.

> Horror shows us our own mortality and lack of control. It makes us admit to our weaknesses and our more secret emotions.

Horror writing works best when it is understated. Whether you're writing gore or nightmare it's better to *suggest* than to be too direct. Many beginners describe streams of blood and splintering bones in elaborate detail. This lacks credibility and doesn't impress anyone. If something is biting your neck, what's more frightening: the blood, which you can't actually see, or the prickling pain and soggy breath around your face?

Suggesting horror in your story

One of the best ways to create fear is to use subtle suggestions, rather than direct statements. If your character is afraid you could say: 'John was afraid, he was really scared', but this doesn't work well. It's better to show the physical experience of fear. 'John felt his heart slam against his ribs, and his stomach liquefied.' This works, but the problem is that it's a horror cliché. So although you must avoid making direct statements, be wary of falling into cliché.

There is still room in horror for occasional vampire and monster stories, if they have a truly original angle, but most horror deals with the ordinary things that frighten us. The key to making a successful story is to take reality and slightly dislocate it. Seeing dark shapes moving just out of sight on a car-park, as you race to get the door open, is more frightening than seeing a vampire flap through the trees. We all know how frightening it can be to be stared at.

- Normal, ordinary fear which reflects our own shortcomings is a good starting point for horror fiction.

Finding your locations

Location is a vital aspect of horror writing. Many of the new writers set their stories in recognisable locations, rather than in graveyards or lonely cottages. The horrors of poverty and loneliness are ideal settings for serious horror fiction, so don't neglect them.

For the fear to be effective your characters must be more than mere victims, so that when the horror affects them the reader will care. Victims make boring characters. Although horror is concerned with weakness, editors don't want stories where the only point is to watch a character get scared and then get killed.

- Make the story relevant to your character's inner motivations.

CHOOSING A GENRE

Although this book is largely concerned with science fiction, the techniques and suggestions also apply to fantasy and horror. You can choose to work in one particular area or, like many of today's writers, you can combine them.

Putting genres together

These days the term science fiction is replaced by **SF** (as opposed to the dated **sci-fi**), because it can also stand for **speculative fiction**, or **slipstream fiction**. It is in these areas, where the genres of science fiction, horror, fantasy, magic realism and the mainstream cross over, that the best work is created.

Many writers have found that:

- science fiction works more effectively if there is a horrific element

- fantasy is more powerful when there is a science fiction idea behind the strange events

- horror can be more credible, when merged with fantasy and science fiction.

By blurring the barrier between genres your fiction can have greater potential.

Choosing a length for your writing

As you develop ideas you will have to decide whether to write:

- short stories
- or novels.

Short stories are sometimes more difficult than novels, but they have the advantage of being quicker to write. You can write ten short stories, improving with every one, in the time it would take you to write half a novel. Short stories also give you more room to experiment with the crossing of genres, finding your own style and developing ideas.

For each idea that you find, determine what sort of a story it could sustain. If the idea is absolutely huge don't spoil it by cramming it into a story. Equally, don't try to spread a small idea through a full-length novel.

> Study novels and stories that you have enjoyed, to judge how ideas relate to the length of a work, and write accordingly.

Creating science fiction

SF is like chemistry, or perhaps even alchemy. All the aspects of your story – the idea, mood, characterisation, theme and plot – must be balanced and must interact perfectly, without clashing, or you'll end up with sludge.

The beauty of science fiction is that you can write about anything that interests you, in almost any way that you like. This doesn't mean you are free to ramble, but if you craft a story well you can tackle any issue or idea that your imagination allows.

Developing your ideas

Your stories may be developed from the concerns of today – medicine, pollution, war, mental health, mutation, and political problems – or you may deal with ideas that are completely new. You have room to experiment with SF. Whatever wonders you feel, whatever confusions distort your life, they can be explored here.

CHECKLIST

- Read plenty of SF, fantasy and horror.

- Become familiar with the latest ideas.

- Learn the clichés, so that you can avoid writing them.

- Try to work out whether a piece is SF, fantasy or horror.

- Find stories where the genres overlap.

- Try to determine what it is about your favourite SF stories that you like.

- Set aside a time and a place to write.

- Try to write something every day, even if only a few lines or notes.

CASE STUDIES

The case studies we will be following through the book show three different approaches to writing science fiction, according to personal taste, experience, available time and lifestyle.

Peter pursues his love of pure SF

Peter, an engineer, is a fan of all kinds of hard science fiction, from the *Star Trek* television series to the novels of Arthur C. Clarke and Stephen Baxter. He wants to write straightforward SF in his spare time, starting with short stories and working up to a novel. Having read SF books for several years he now subscribes to *Interzone* and is familiar with the latest ideas.

Michael's aim is expressing emotion

Michael is an English teacher, with little knowledge of science but a love of characters. He feels that horror can be a fiction of great honesty and humanity, but he also wants to include elements of science fiction and fantasy. His main aim is to express personal emotion, through the heightened realism offered by SF, fantasy and horror, writing short stories for small-press magazines.

Ruth wants to experiment

Ruth is a university student who wants to write experimental science fiction and fantasy in her spare time. Starting with short stories she eventually wants to write a novel combining SF, fantasy and horror, to create original effects.

DISCUSSION POINTS

1. Imagine yourself in a familiar place, such as a café, but two hundred years into the future. How different would you be and how would you act?

2. What frightens you? Make a list of times you were frightened, and see how much this was affected by your imagination, your senses and the actual events.

3. Do you prefer to read SF, fantasy or horror? Which would you prefer to write? How can you use combinations of all three to strengthen your ideas?

2
Finding Ideas

GETTING TO GRIPS WITH IDEAS

Ideas are the driving force of science fiction. Whatever your background and knowledge you can learn to create original story ideas.

When you think of science fiction classics, such as *Star Trek*, you may wonder how to come up with such vast ideas. The imagined worlds are so rich, complete and well thought out that it seems a daunting task. The good news is that nobody comes up with vast ideas in an instant.

The imagined world of *Star Trek* developed slowly, from a few core ideas. The idea of the *Starship Enterprise* itself led naturally to the invention of phasers, transporter beams, energy shields and Klingons. If the first idea is strong enough, it will create a universe.

When setting out, don't try to create whole worlds at once. Your job at this stage is to find core ideas, and the best way is by making notes.

Making Notes

Carry a notebook and pen with you at all times and get used to taking notes. Make sure the notebook fits into your pocket easily, and that your pen works freely.

Your aim is to

● observe
● and record.

By looking at the world, and noting your observations, you will find that ideas occur without effort.

When taking notes there are four main rules:

1. Write thoughts down immediately, or they will be forgotten.

2. Don't be embarrassed about writing in public.

3. Forget about grammar and spelling.

4. Don't wait for big ideas, just observe and record.

You are the only person who will ever read your notes, so they can be scruffy and badly written. If an idea seems less than perfect, or poorly expressed, don't worry, just get the words down. There will be time for editing later. The important point is to record your observations.

Knowing what to write

Try to observe any unusual sensations. You should use all your senses: sound, smell, touch and taste are as important as sight. Anything that stimulates your senses should be noted, whether it be the colour of a squashed kiwi fruit on the pavement, or the smell of an office when everybody has gone home. If you notice it, write it down.

You should also be aware of:

● unusual phrases and names
● possible locations and settings for stories
● interesting people and their reactions
● questions that come into your mind.

In short, note down anything strange or appealing that catches your attention. In all cases, concentrate on *detail*. When noting the sounds in a café, for example, don't write 'café sounds', but describe the steaming cappuccino machine, scraping chairs, even the sound of rain thrown against the window.

You can take notes at any spare moment, when something comes to mind.

Don't judge your thoughts before writing them down; always get the idea onto paper immediately.

Many new writers think they should wait for grand ideas or moving images before noting anything, but the opposite is true.

You should make an abundance of notes, recording every moment of interest in your day. This creates a fertile source material for idea generation.

ASKING 'WHAT IF?'

Science fiction has been described as the fiction of *what if*? By asking this question you will come up with the best ideas. What if the world was struck by a meteor? What if the aliens landed? What if computers had minds of their own? By asking questions you can turn your ordinary notes into solid science fiction ideas.

Developing your notes

Read through your notes frequently. Find sections that interest you and use them as starting points for ideas. A sample page of notes, taken over the course of an afternoon, could be something like this:

'Two women on the train are wearing the same perfume. Certain smells remind me of places and people. Imagine somebody I don't like wearing my girlfriend's perfume. How would it make me feel? The man across from me has a cold. His hands are covered in gold rings. He rubs his fingers all the time. Are his rings important, do they hold some memory for him? He's picking his nails. Keeps blowing his nose. I don't want to catch what he's got.'

At present these notes don't mean much, but they could easily be developed into science fiction ideas, by asking 'what if?' From the above notes it is natural to ask, 'What if scent was used to create emotion? What if objects could store human memory?'

Letting your thoughts lead you
Write down the most important points and expand them with more detail. Again, you will be the only person to read these notes, so don't aim for perfection. Experiment with the ideas and see where your thoughts lead you. Be daring and follow strange thoughts, no matter how outrageous they may seem at first. If you feel a scene developing, or if your imagination goes in a new direction, follow it.

● Write about your notes and ideas will develop.

Creating a universe

The smallest notes can lead to the greatest ideas. For example, the note about storing human memory in objects could be developed in many ways. The result might be a short story about a new type of bio-metallic compound which records memory. This metal could be fashioned into wedding rings and used at a marriage ceremony to share memories. A different approach would be to show one person developing this memory technology in secret, and using it for deceit or revenge. Perhaps by giving the rings away he could steal memories from people.

The idea could be taken much further, by asking more questions. If objects could store our thoughts, would people sell their favourite memories? Would people become addicted to the past? Might there be a black market for memory ornaments? Would people confuse their own past with that of others? These questions bring up problems, such as where would the bio-metal come from, how would memories be put into it, who would control the process? By asking these questions you can create an entire reality. Your imagined world will have its own people, culture, economy, religion and lifestyle. The perfect place to set your story.

> By observing the world, and imagining how it could be different, you will create science fiction ideas.

As your future world, alien planet or alternate reality comes into shape, you will create more detail than could ever be used in a story. This is good, because notes are never wasted. If you are aware of background detail it will give your story a realistic feel.

Reading for inspiration

You don't have to be a scientist to think of good ideas. The knowledge you need can easily be gained from science fiction and science fact. By immersing yourself in other people's ideas, and asking 'what if?', you will find inspiration.

It is important to read plenty of science fiction, so that you can find out which ideas have already been used. You will find stories in magazines such as *Interzone* and *The Third Alternative*, and every bookshop and library has a large science fiction section. This reading should ideally be supplemented by:

- popular science journals such as *New Scientist* and *Focus*
- paranormal magazines, including *Fortean Times* and *Nexus*
- books on any aspect of science, technology or culture that interests you.

If you find these heavy going, remember that your every-day reading can be a source of ideas.

- An article about ordinary events can lead to something more bizarre, if you use your imagination.

- The *way* you read is as important as *what* you read.

- Keep your notebook handy, ask '*what if?*' as you read, and write down your thoughts.

COMBINING CONCEPTS

The best way to create a stunning idea is to combine two ordinary ideas. This is a trick used by most science fiction writers, and helps to make the most of your notes.

The example notes shown earlier suggested several ideas about memory objects, chemical emotions and people giving off scents. There was also mention of infection and disease. By putting some of these together the ideas are transformed into something fantastic. Imagine if people gave off smells which reflected the way they were feeling. Perhaps these scents could induce the same emotion in those who smell them. Sadness might spread like a plague. Love could be bottled. The resulting confusion would make people question their feelings, and the strain on relationships would be fascinating.

By combining concepts your ideas become more complex and original, suggesting possibilities that would be difficult to think up on their own. If an idea appeals to you, but doesn't quite suggest a story, combine it with something else, no matter how ordinary, and see where it takes you.

Expanding scenes

As your ideas grow, try writing a scene which could be part of the story. Don't spend too much time thinking about this. Simply write it. You only have to write a few lines. Even if you don't know what the story is about, how it will end or who the characters will be, start writing a scene. Imagine one person, in one situation, and write.

With the above example you might imagine a person feeling emotions for somebody she has never met. She might feel in love. You could write about her reactions as she tries to hide this from her partner.

In some cases you will find that the story begins to write itself. If not, don't worry. The scenes you write now may or may not end up in the story. All that matters is that you get used to the imaginary world, watching your ideas develop. Don't worry about the exact wording yet, and forget about grammar. Get on with the writing and watch the idea grow.

To make this process easier:

● Avoid writing a whole history; concentrate on a few minutes of the character's life.

● Imagine how you would feel in this situation and write this into your character.

● Use more than one character, because interaction is always more interesting.

● Give your characters names, for added realism.

TESTING YOUR IDEAS

Some science fiction ideas are huge, concerning space, time and the nature of existence. Other ideas deal with small matters, such as the effect of technology on personal relationships. Both approaches to science fiction are valid, so don't be put off if your ideas seem too large or too small.

Having created ideas that excite you, and written a few scenes, it is time to test your idea. Ask yourself these questions:

● Would it interest me, if somebody else wrote it?
● Is it original?
● Is it believable?

If the answer to all three questions is yes, you are ready to develop the story in full.

If you find yourself worrying about the last question, remember that a good writer can make unbelievable ideas acceptable.

> When asking yourself if a story is believable, decide whether it *feels* believable to you, rather than if it *is* actually possible.

The idea of an alien race which only sleeps once a year, although extremely peculiar, is acceptable. A story about humans learning to download their memories into computers, although highly unlikely, does feel believable.

If an idea isn't working, or doesn't seem quite right yet, accept that it may need further development and put it to one side. Never throw your notes away, because one day they will prove useful. For now, keep writing and get as many ideas as possible onto paper. Before long you'll be ready to write your first science fiction story.

CHECKLIST

- Buy plenty of notebooks and pens, and use them frequently.

- Read through your notes and develop them.

- Cut out newspaper and magazine articles which interest you.

- Read as much as possible, noting your thoughts.

- Ask yourself 'what if?' as often as possible.

- Link some of your ideas together and see where this leads.

- As your imaginary world develops, picture the people who might live there.

- Throw nothing away. Every note could prove useful.

CASE STUDIES

Peter asks 'what if?'
At work Peter has to study technical engineering manuals. While reading about pump valves he makes notes about artificial heart

valves. That night he spends an hour developing his notes. By asking 'what if?' he wonders if valves could be applied to human thoughts. What if the government of the future used valves to seal off unwanted thoughts? Or perhaps individuals could use neural valves, to shut off the past. Peter writes a scene in which a man persuades a surgeon to insert a brain valve to repress painful memories. This is a good starting point for his story.

Michael combines ideas

During his school day Michael takes notes whenever possible. He notes the way his class becomes restless at the same time every day, when the sun gets in their eyes. On the train journey home he notes how the warm weather makes him feel lonely. In a spare hour Michael goes through his notes, but none of the ideas particularly appeal to him. To solve the dilemma he combines two ordinary ideas. 'What if' he writes, 'people experienced loneliness at certain times of the day or year? What if, as the sun went down each day, there was one hour in which everybody felt a need to be with others?' He reads through the rest of his notes, adding thoughts, before setting his work aside.

Ruth sets the scene

During college lectures Ruth supplements her essay notes with story ideas. She observes the strutting lecturer, and writes a description of his face and beard. When he talks about lens refraction Ruth makes notes about the way solid objects can bend light, to project a distant image. It occurs to her that a lens could be used to project the mind out of the body. At the weekend she sets an afternoon aside for writing. She writes a scene in which a scientist, based on her lecturer, uses a focused beam of light to move his mind. Things go wrong when his mind is projected into a wall, or an animal, or another person. Perhaps the lens could also be used to read minds or to influence people? Ruth sees that her character will determine the direction of this story, and decides to develop him in detail before writing the story.

DISCUSSION POINTS

1. During the next few hours make notes about anything that catches your attention. Why is it important to make so many notes?

2. Reading through your notes, pick some interesting points and ask 'what if?' How does this help to create ideas?

3. Take two ideas, no matter how ordinary they seem, and combine them. How can this help to create an imaginary world?

4. Imagine a scene from your story and begin writing, relating it to your ideas. Why does this help with story development?

3
Putting Your Ideas on Paper

FINDING A THEME

With some of your ideas worked out you may want to launch in and write the first page, as shown later, but you might need to do some more groundwork first.

Your research, preparation and notes are all part of the story-writing process. The more work you do now, the easier it will be to get into the story. When writers are faced with a blank page, many freeze and experience writer's block. It is common to feel a complete inability to write. By working with SF ideas, scenes, images and feelings in the early stages you will avoid this problem. When you are faced with a blank page you will be ready to write.

One of the best ways to give your science fiction cohesion and direction is to choose a **theme** before you begin writing. A theme is the core idea that drives your story. One of your main aims when writing is to reveal this theme.

> Every scene, line of dialogue and image will contribute to the expression of your theme.

Although stories communicate images, scenes and emotions, the overall effect is to communicate the underlying theme.

In some cases your writing will evolve as you work, often quite unexpectedly. For this reason it is safe to begin writing a story without any idea of the exact theme, if you feel certain that the ideas are strong enough. As you write you discover the theme. In most cases, however, it is wise to explore your ideas first, to see what theme they are leading to.

Choosing a theme

Themes can sometimes be summed up with one or two words, such as death, regret or jealousy. Any aspect of existence that can be summed up briefly could be called a theme. Whatever your story is *really* about can be called your theme.

In reality the themes are more complicated, because a story would never be simply about death. It would be about the death of a friend, or the death of parents, for example. In this way the events of your story dictate the exact shading of the theme. There are millions of different viewpoints of death, and all could be used to create a story. So, when exploring your theme, resist the temptation to label with one word.

Using SF to take themes further
In SF, fantasy and horror you have the opportunity to take themes much further than usual. Instead of writing about familiar forms of death, you could write about suspended animation, partial brain death, or storing human memory on computer chips after death. Here, the SF ideas dictate themes which could not be explored by any other type of fiction. This is the strength of SF and something you should always aim to exploit.

Referring to your ideas
Your theme is much more than an idea: it is the overall picture. When asking 'what if?' to find ideas, the theme will often slot into place. What if somebody regretted actions that happened in a dream, or during a virtual reality adventure? What if these regrets were more substantial than the events in their real life? What if somebody was jealous of an artificial intelligence? By taking on these more bizarre themes you are still looking at death, regret, jealousy or whatever other themes you come across, but you are looking at them in a new way.

Ideas are only part of the story. The idea of storing memories on organic computer chips can be used to explore themes of mortality, insecurity, death, regret and many others. It all depends on the way your story develops.

● The idea is a starting point, and it is the characters and events of the story that will dictate what the story is about.

Although we can label themes approximately, to explain a theme fully would take more than a few lines; it will take an entire story.

This is why we write. Although a theme could be summed up as The Nature of True Love, simply writing this down communicates nothing. By writing a story in which the characters meet, argue, split up and then discover their true feelings, we understand the theme fully.

> In science fiction the use of extreme ideas will allow you to communicate extremely complex, challenging original themes.

WRITING YOUR FIRST PAGE

Writing the first page of any story is daunting, and the best way to avoid the fear is to realise that your story was begun a long time ago. During your note-taking you probably wrote lines and images that will appear on the first page. You have been writing notes for some time and now you are simply putting everything into place.

Rewriting is a major part of the creative process, so don't be afraid of making mistakes. You can correct them later. For now get words on to paper, to see how the story develops. Write freely and steadily, without too much worry about style, grammar, or the sound of sentences. You will make mistakes, but it is important to correct them after you have written a few pages, rather than the moment they are written.

- Write first and edit afterwards. This allows you to create freely, without stumbling.

- Examine the ideas you have created so far and try to get a feeling for possible themes.

- Remember to tie the ideas to the scenes and characters you have explored so far, and let the story suggest a theme.

- Work through your notes, adding new details to get a much better picture of the story.

Choosing a starting point

Having written plenty of notes you need to determine a **starting point** for your story. Even if you don't know exactly what will

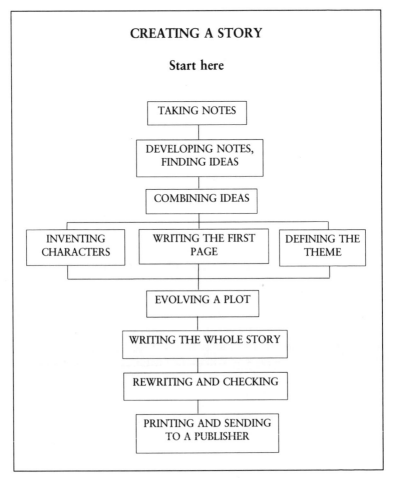

Fig. 1. The process of story creation.

happen, who all the characters will be, or the exact workings of your imagined universe, you have to start somewhere.

Writing the first line
The first line of any story should be:

- compelling
- unusual
- attention grabbing.

In SF a first line can dictate the entire tone, style and approach of a story. It is vital that you find a line which sets the story up in this way. If you worry about that now, however, you will never get the story written. Instead of trying to find a perfect first line, get straight into the writing, as described below, and come back to the opening paragraph. Once you know more about the story it will be much easier to find a good first line.

Concentrating on the action

A good story will usually show the most important events from a character's life. It will show a time of great change and conflict. Your character will have to battle with internal problems, such as fear or jealousy, in order to solve external problems, such as being hunted by a killer android or escaping from the Thought Police.

To find the ideal starting point try to begin the story as close to the vital events as possible, just before the major change takes place. If the story is about Jed experimenting with a new kinetic drug, and unravelling a mystery from his past, begin the story just before he obtains the drug. Although build-up is important you shouldn't spend pages and pages showing Jed's ordinary life, having breakfast, travel-matting to work, networking his brain to the office computer and so on. Some normality is required, to make the contrast meaningful, but do begin the story close to the important change.

It is important to strike balance here. Although the first page should interest readers, avoid letting off too many fireworks straight away. If there are lots of explosions, hover-car chases and phaser battles on page one, the drama won't interest the reader if they don't know what the character is like. So although you should begin close to the key change and action, you also need to establish *who* the character is and make the reader care for your character. This will be explored in more detail later, but for now you need to choose a moment when the story can begin, to write the first page.

Revealing vital information

The first page should ideally reveal who, why, what, where and when.

- Who is the story about?
- Why is it happening to them?
- Why is it so important?

- What is actually going on in the story?
- Where is the action taking place?
- When is the action taking place?

Although stories are about gradual revelations of information, with new twists and discoveries, it is important to know the above factors on the first page. If you write a description of your character, her problems, and what is going on, but neglect to mention the time or location, your reader will not have the full picture. If you then go on to mention her walking down to the beach house, and looking up at the moon, your reader may be puzzled because it is just as likely your character was walking through London at midday.

SHOWING THE STORY

Instead of explaining what is going on, and who is involved, *show* the reader the story. By describing your character interacting with other people in different locations you will convey all the necessary information. One of the best rules to follow is:

- show, don't tell.

Instead of telling us that she is on the beach, show her running her hands through the sand nervously, muttering to herself about her boss. Don't say that she is unhappy, show her frown and reveal her unhappy thoughts. Don't tell us she is cold, but show her tightening her cardigan against the wind. By showing the reader you avoid stalling to explain. This is the basis of good fiction. Avoid direct statements and show us what is going on. Reveal who is there, what they are doing, why it matters. Show us where the action is and when it is taking place.

> In their haste to reveal ideas, characters and stories, SF writers tend to over-explain, which spoils the story. When writing your first page, get into the habit of revealing information by *showing* us what happens.

Imagining fiction

Although fiction may seem dauntingly complex there is a simple technique which helps everything to slot into place. Imagination.

By imagining a scene before you write it, and while you write about it, you will automatically test the realism of scenes. You will also be using a more creative thought process. Trying to think up stories and plots through reasoning can be counter-creative. An over-analytical approach may force you to discount ideas through logic, before you have played with them creatively.

Although logical thought is important, to make sure that ideas work, that a plot is plausible and that your story makes sense, simply trying to think up ideas is a huge task. If you begin a scene with one line, and then try to think of the next, it is extremely difficult. If you write one line, and then imagine what happens next, it is much easier. Having imagined the next event, you write about it.

This subtle difference in approach to fiction can solve many writing problems, and helps with the delicate world-building mentioned in Chapter 1. When writing your first page, instead of trying to work out what would happen next, what your next line should be or whether you are revealing the right amount of information, simply imagine the scene. Imagine your character in the invented world, interacting with other people, and describe what you see.

Enjoying experimenting

As ever, don't be afraid to experiment. You will probably write several versions of your first page and that can only be a good thing. At this point be relaxed about writing different versions. As time goes by you will need to experiment less and first-draft pages will be closer to perfection.

CHECKLIST

● Work out what your story is really about.

● Make sure your ideas and themes are linked.

● Consider what type of characters will best explore your theme.

● Imagine the action, dialogue and images before writing.

● Write several versions of the first page.

● Rewrite the page, using the 'show, don't tell' principle.

● Check to see if you are revealing who, why, what, where and when.

CASE STUDIES

Peter tries out a theme
After reviewing his notes Peter feels that his story will be about repression. He wants to write about the way people create an illusion of control by ignoring problems. He creates a character, Brian, who is wounded by a past relationship and tries to purchase a brain valve on the black market. In the first scene he shows memories intruding into Brian's mind as he talks to the surgeon. Strangely, the pain of the memories is almost pleasant and Brian isn't sure how to proceed. This isn't exactly what Peter had planned, but it may offer even more scope to express his theme so it is something he can work with.

Michael adapts his ideas
Looking back at the idea of periodic cycles of loneliness, Michael realises that his theme will be the way loneliness affects behaviour. He imagines a character who tries to ignore loneliness, but frequently succumbs to it, acting in socially dangerous ways. Unsure of the full details, he writes several versions of the first page. His main character, Liam Anderson, is trying to get home from work before the loneliness (caused by some effect he has yet to establish) sets in. Michael has shown his character's appearance and mannerisms, the futuristic world he lives in and his fear of loneliness.

Ruth writes the first page
Ruth realises that her character must be self-involved, to keep his invention secret, so her theme will be about selfishness. She imagines the character perfecting the machine, with the sole intent of influencing the mind of the woman he loves. She has shown no interest in him and he plans to use the projector to change her mind. Set in a future Oxford University, her first page reveals a

place where astonishing technology clashes with old-world styles and attitudes. The moody atmosphere of the location contrasts with the desperation of her main character.

DISCUSSION POINTS

1. Look back at some of your favourite stories and novels, and determine their themes. How is theme established in the first few pages?

2. What is the difference between the ideas and the theme in a story? How will this affect what you write?

3. Look at first lines from your favourite SF stories and novels. How do they capture your attention and contribute to the story?

4. Look at first pages from SF stories. Do they hold your attention as well as conveying relevant information? How quickly and effectively do SF writers convey the 'world view'?

4
Creating People

DISCOVERING CHARACTERS

Whatever type of story you write, whether personal, global or universal, your characters will bring it to life. In SF, fantasy and horror characters can include **androids, aliens** and **computers**, as well as humans. It is the way these characters interact and develop that will express the ideas and themes of your story.

If, for example, your idea concerns the effect of emotion-drugs, the interest doesn't lie in government reports, lab tests or theoretical arguments. The real interest lies in the way such drugs could affect people. By showing one or two characters dealing with this problem, your story will reflect the way it could affect a whole society.

Inventing people

Sometimes your story will arise from a fully-imagined character. Your notes and research will lead you to imagine one person, and the story, idea and theme will relate to this character.

With most stories, however, you will find the idea, theme and setting before you have any firm characters in mind.

Whether your characters are clear in your mind, or completely absent, the following techniques will help you to create more realistic people. You can spend either a few seconds, or a few hours, working on these initial stages. For a short story only a few minutes' work will be required. You will always find out more about a character from the actual writing, so this preparation, although detailed, should be brief and inspirational.

> Use your imagination, find the answers as rapidly as possible and let the story do the rest of the work.

When you are used to creating characters, having written several stories, you will learn to cut out much of this preparation, but it is the best way to learn. It will help you during periods of confused and uncertain writing.

When inventing characters, you must determine:

- name
- age
- sex
- appearance
- temperament
- religion
- employment
- social class
- birthplace/nationality.

In terms of SF you may also have to decide:

- race (alien, human, android)
- language spoken
- special abilities and needs (such as psychic powers, breathing chlorine, feeding on light)
- origins (Earth or elsewhere).

These are the absolute basics, that provide a skeleton for you to work with.

Making a character unique

To make a character unique you must generate a complex and realistic personality. Think about your character and determine his or her preferences in terms of:

- entertainment
- food
- habits
- terms of expression
- favourite places
- special memories
- hobbies
- education.

You can also determine whether your character prefers company or solitude, cities or countryside, flying or driving, argument or compromise. You should establish a history for each character, with any questions that come to mind, writing notes about their past relationships. Ask yourself how a character feels about:

- parents
- close friends
- childhood
- partnerships and marriage
- politics.

Finding the soul of a character

There are three questions which will help you to gain insight into your character.

- What annoys, elates, depresses or uplifts your character?

- What is your character afraid of?

- What secrets does your character withhold?

The character you develop at this stage will help you when you come to write. Many of these details will never be printed, but they will help you to understand how your character will change and react. You are also free to change these details later. If you find that your dominant character is actually submissive, using control as a front, you can change your approach. Finding out about character in this way is half the fun of writing. In SF, fantasy and horror the secret and hidden aspects of characters are often the most fascinating, so expect surprises.

Setting your character in a context

A fully imagined character does not exist in isolation. Like people in the real world, characters exist in a time, a place and in relation to other people. To fully understand your character you must understand *where* they are, and *who* they relate to.

When developing your character remember that most of them will be brought together at some point. It is the way these individuals respond to each other that will provide the friction and harmony which creates emotion for the reader.

NAMING CHARACTERS

Imagine seeing *Star Wars* for the first time and finding out the evil ruler of the Empire was called Kevin. In fact he was known as Darth Vadar, a name which emanates hostility and evil. Names should suit the people they represent and, where possible, they should be original.

Surnames can make an ordinary name more original. There are millions of Pams and Jacks in the world, but there will be few people called Pam Stuyvesat or Jack Stone. Give a character a more interesting name and you give readers something to remember them by. Think of Jean-Luc Picard, Luke Skywalker, and even Duncan McLeod, and you can see how a strong name works. A complete name is also easy to remember and makes your character a more rounded individual.

In science fiction your names will often be more unusual than Bob and Sarah. Even so, names such as Tqyrnx and Fgrurta are difficult to pronounce and can annoy readers. Names such as Odo, Quark and Dax sound alien without being too obscure.

Looking for new names

Most science fiction writers use place names listed in a world atlas to help with ideas. For each story you can choose one region and let all your names be based on places within it. This regional flavour to your names helps to add extra realism. If the names aren't quite what you want, shift letters and look for word combinations that are more suitable.

Choose a name that suits the person's cultural background, and remember that in conversation nicknames or shortened names will often be used. These show the way that other people within a story think of your character, and are an effective way of revealing the state of relationships without direct exposition. Never forget the character's reaction to their own name; it can be revealing.

If one character is called Peter, avoid calling another Petra, or confusion can result. Each name should be simple to read and distinguish.

●   Without names your characters are only ideas. Give them good names and you turn them into people.

STRENGTHENING CHARACTERS

By developing the people of your fiction, as described, you may stumble across a key characteristic which gives your character true definition.

> Although characters are complex each will have a key characteristic, one aspect of their personality, which says more about them than anything else.

This characteristic will tie in with your theme and ideas. If your story concerns the effects of a false-memory virus, exploring the theme of emotional illusions, the character's key characteristic could be an inability to face up to the past. Whatever else the person may be like, in terms of mood, preferences and appearance, this inability to accept past mistakes and events will drive all the main decisions and actions.

Finding the key characteristic

The key characteristic is often determined by a character's yearning. A character who is content and at one with the world will not be interesting. Readers want to read about characters with flaws and unfulfilled desires. It is the way a character acts to deal with flaws, and to bring about change, that makes a story compelling. A lonely character, yearning for love, or a married character yearning for separation, is more interesting than one who is happily married with no problems.

When creating your character, ask yourself what your character *really wants*. The answer will help you to understand this person's main driving force.

Going beyond the obvious

Note that the character's main aim and key characteristic can be opposed to each other. A key characteristic may be abruptness, while the main aim may be to establish friendship. The story will explore how these two must be balanced for the character to satisfy the yearning.

A key characteristic can be a burden, or an aspect of the personality that requires expression. In Geoff Ryman's *The Child Garden* for instance, Milena's key characteristic is a fierce individuality, which makes her lonely. Rather than suppressing her individuality, she develops it, and is thus able to form the first meaningful relationship in her life. The end result is that by being fiercely individual she learns to express universal emotions.

Writing about change
SF is about change and development. External problems must be dealt with, but for real change to take place something must change within the character. So if one character wants to find love, she may have to learn to control anger. There is always a trade-off, to achieve balance, and it should never be easy. Your story should be about the most important moments, difficult decisions and painful actions in a character's life.

PUTTING CHARACTERS INTO ACTION

Once you begin to form your story you will have to decide:

- who the main character will be
- how many characters the story requires
- what the main relationships are
- whether to use first or third person
- which viewpoint will be used.

All stories require at least one character, but most contain two or more so that some sense of relationship can be shown. In some novels there are hundreds of characters.

A character isn't simply a person who you invent. A character is a person in a specific situation. In SF this is more important than usual, because the SF situation dictates exactly how the character must act and respond. When inventing characters you are creating people in situations.

Working with a viewpoint character
The viewpoint character is the person whose eyes we see the story through. In first-person fiction one character describes the action as a memory.

'I walked into the first decontamination chamber with Sasha behind me. Sniffing the cold air, I detected a whiff of salt.'

In the third person you describe the action more remotely.

'Jared walked into the decontamination chamber, with Sasha behind him. Sniffing the air, he detected a whiff of salt.'

Before you begin writing, decide whether to use first or third person. Both forms are equally useful in science fiction, with first person providing an intimate approach and third person a more steady tone. Bear in mind that if your character dies at the end of the book it will be difficult to justify first person.

Choosing a viewpoint

In both the above examples the viewpoint belongs to one character, Jared. We see the story via the perceptions of one person. If Sasha had detected the smell of salt that would have been a viewpoint shift, which would sound wrong to the reader. Whether you use first or third person you should describe the action from the viewpoint of one character at a time.

Shifting the viewpoint

In longer, structured, works you can shift viewpoint, from chapter to chapter, but you must do so consistently. If Sasha has three viewpoint chapters, so should Jared and Breena.

Within each chapter use one viewpoint, showing only the action that the character could perceive. Never reveal information that the character isn't aware of, such as 'Behind the wall a Basking Troll was waiting for him, but he had no idea it was there, and walked into its path.' If he doesn't know, we shouldn't either. Only when he sees the troll leaping at his face should the reader find out.

Being consistent

Equally, you can only show the thoughts and speculations of the viewpoint character. If you are using Jared's viewpoint, you can describe his feelings and thoughts, but nobody else's. Although he may believe that Sasha is confused or upset, based on her expressions, actions and dialogue, he can never be certain. It is acceptable to switch to her viewpoint in a separate chapter, but when writing from his viewpoint stick to it.

Viewpoint switches are tempting at times, but they weaken characterisation. Readers like to get inside the minds of individual characters, so you write from one viewpoint at a time.

Making characters distinctive

The background work you have performed, building up an impression of the characters, will help you to describe them. If you imagine clearly, your descriptions of them should make them distinctive. If three characters are in the room, your aim as a writer is to make the reader imagine each person clearly. Every word of dialogue, every movement, reaction, expression and gesture, should be distinctive.

When revealing characteristics avoid making statements. The worst sort of writing consists of 'Karen was angry.' The way to reveal a character is through action and perception. It will take several scenes, perhaps, to reveal that Karen is determined, perhaps showing her in dangerous situations (with people or machinery). This will create a better effect than simply stating that she is determined. To reveal that she is angry, show her face reddening. 'Karen looked down, knowing that her face was going red.'

Reveal character without statements, by showing how people act, interact, and how they think, feel and perceive. Don't say, he was a worried man, show him worrying.

Be consistent. If a character refuses to make eye contact on page one, don't show him gazing into somebody's eyes later on. Change in a character will occur, but such change should be progressive so that it is believable.

DEALING WITH ALIEN CHARACTERS

When you come to describe non-human characters, whether they be aliens or androids, special care is needed. For the reader to identify with aliens they must have traits that are recognisable to us. In many cases these traits are exaggerated, as with the warlike Klingons of *Star Trek*.

Your aliens shouldn't simply be humans with different anatomy.

- To make aliens interesting they should be *truly* alien, perhaps with different methods of eating, breathing, reproducing and even thinking.

- Their perception of the known senses may be greater or more limited than ours.

- They may perceive senses we are unaware of.

- Sometimes they will have abilities beyond ours.

- In other cases concepts such as love will be a complete mystery to them.

It is this slurring of characteristics within aliens that gives you such potential for creativity.

Your aliens offer room for experiment, but they should arise from the demands of the story and fit in with your world view. If you are writing about an android slave trade between Earth, the Mars Colony and the planet Hedrall 4 you will have to invent human characters, Mars colonists and Hedrallians, and even the androids themselves.

Making aliens distinctive

Once you have invented a race of aliens you have to invent the individual characters. Just as every human is unique, all your aliens should be unique. Although there will be general traits, preferences, requirements and abilities, each individual will differ within those parameters.

Avoid making all your aliens identical in nature, because such generalisations are never plausible or enjoyable. In *Star Trek: The Next Generation* much of the interest arose from seeing Commander Worf fight against the anger of his Klingon personality, while retaining his cultural heritage. This type of conflict within aliens often makes them more interesting than if they are 'typical' Hedrallians.

Understanding the aliens' home world

> To fully understand your alien characters, you should understand the workings of their home world.

If your story is set in an alien's home world this will be no problem, as your general world-building will reveal the necessary details.

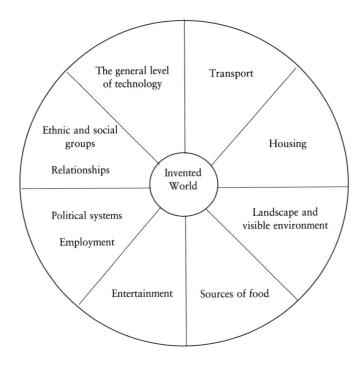

Fig. 2. The elements of world building.

If the aliens are away from their home world you should still keep their origins in mind.

When we know nothing of a race, other than its appearance and actions, it is truly alien. When we learn about a home world, with its culture, economics, religion and social structure, we come to understand a race. Many stories and novels have been concerned solely with this discovery of an alien heritage.

Even if the readers never see the aliens home world, spend some time making notes about it so that you understand how and where your aliens live.

CHECKLIST

● Are your characters all distinctive?

- Can you imagine how your characters will respond to each other?

- Are your characters' names easy to read and remember?

- Do you have enough characters to create sufficient tension?

- Is there room in your story to give each character full expression?

- Be aware of your characters' appearance.

- Know the characters' full background.

- Determine each person's key characteristic.

CASE STUDIES

Peter invents characters

Peter realises that his main character, Brian, could be pathetic if he simply wants to hide from his past. To solve this Peter makes Brian a struggling, yet talented, pianist. He is trying to suppress painful memories, believing that personal misery is spoiling his piano performances. To make this more interesting Brian will be somebody who takes criticism well in public, but is mortified by it in private. Perhaps the painful memories involve his closest friend admitting that she doesn't think he is a good pianist. Peter determines that Brian's key characteristic is a desire to be liked, through his art. Peter also outlines the friend and the surgeon, writing brief descriptions and scenes of interaction.

Michael finds the right people

Michael has already established that Liam Anderson's key characteristic is a fear of loneliness. To make this more interesting he wants to make Liam into a character unable to face up to this. He will try to live in isolation, refusing to let people close, finding that the Loneliness Hour always destroys him bit by bit. To add poignancy Michael writes a scene which involves Liam's sister trying to get close to him. He realises that several characters could be trying to get close to Liam, which will add irony and pain to the story. After writing several scenes Michael considers switching the viewpoint, to make Veronica the key character, but realises there is more interest if the reader identifies with Liam.

Ruth gives her character more depth

Ruth develops her characters, by inventing full backgrounds for each. To avoid turning the professor into a cliché (eccentric, mad) she makes him appear ordinary, under-dressing. His best friends are factory workers, with whom he spends his evenings, though he doesn't admit this to his colleagues. When writing about Elissa, the woman desired by the professor, Ruth realises she will be more interesting if she contains a contradiction. On the surface she can be angelic and calm, but her secret nature could be much darker. This factor alone will affect the story, because the professor is only looking at the surface.

DISCUSSION POINTS

1. Imagine all of your main characters in one scene. How do they feel about each other? Can you tell them apart easily?

2. Who is the viewpoint character? Try writing the scene from several different viewpoints and see how this affects the story.

3. What is the main relationship between your characters? How does this reflect your idea and theme? How can it be developed?

4. How does situation affect character? Put one or more characters into different situations (such as escape, imprisonment, first meeting). How does this affect their interaction?

5
Evolving Your Plot

LETTING CHARACTERS CREATE YOUR STORY

Plot is a series of events that takes the story from beginning to end. You show the reader segments of an imagined reality, which relate to each other in a logical manner. Eventually these sections of imagined life create meaning and emotion, and tell a character's story.

Plot is the structure that turns situation into story.

'Bellan tried a new emotion-drug' is a situation, whereas 'Bellan tried a new emotion-drug, because he wanted to forget his past relationships' is a story. So the plot of this story might be 'Bellan steals the drug. He fights his urge to take it. He argues with a friend about it. He takes the drug. He deals with its consequences.' The plot has evolved from the character situation, the theme and the intended emotion. When fleshed out with full scenes, character interaction and imagery, this will be a story.

Deciding what happens next

Whenever you find an idea it will probably be a situation which needs turning into a story. Although some writers like to plan a plot, you do not need to be so mechanical. It can be just as satisfying to start with a problem and begin writing.

Plot arose in fiction as a way of keeping readers interested, and of handling time. As such plot is a tool, not a restrictive rule. It is something you can use to make a story better, but it should never be your master. If the plot takes over you may force your characters into incongruous situations and lose track of your theme. Keep your eyes on the logic of plot, but don't let a desire for more drama force you into finding extreme plots. The relevance of a plot to your characters, theme and story is more important than plotting a complex series of events for the sake of it.

Using plot creatively

J. R. R. Tolkien's *Lord of the Rings* contains a stunning plot, but Tolkien let the story evolve as he wrote, without any idea of where it was going. The shock he felt, as he made important and frightening discoveries, was passed on to the readers. He backed characters into corners, making the situation as difficult as possible so that the story would demand an important plot twist. If he'd tried to plan plots before writing he may have dismissed risky ideas as being unworkable.

Although plot is usually defined as the plan of events in a narrative or drama, planning is not necessary. In science fiction, fantasy and horror it does help, however, if you understand the logical direction of your fiction before you begin.

Adding the dramatic elements

The best drama occurs through character interaction. You don't need overt drama, but *something* must happen.

A story usually opens with a conflict. Your story will concern the most important events in the character's life, a situation that requires response and character action. Fiction is all about response to situation. If Bellan takes the emotion-drugs, and finds that he is losing precious memories, the plot demands that he do something about this. Rather than sitting there and thinking 'Oh dear', he must try to resolve the situation. Perhaps he will seek help from another person, take another drug, or experiment with telepathy techniques he learnt as a child. Whatever you decide, he must do something.

Bringing in action

If you find that a character does too much thinking, you may have created a non-starter. Readers don't want to know about pure victims – those who sit back while the world happens to them – they want to read about people who fight conflict and drive the narrative.

The balance between victim and action is a delicate one. Your character must be a victim of circumstance, whether caused from within or without, otherwise there is no conflict. A pure victim, however, is not interesting. This doesn't mean that all stories must have happy endings, where the character's actions pay off. It means that stories are about the actions of your characters, in response to conflict. By detailing events that a character brings about, in the face of a conflict, you create a plot.

STRENGTHENING THE PLOT

The best plots work in two ways:

- they get worse
- they force the character to change.

If the worst moment happens at the beginning, and things gradually get better, the reader will feel that something has gone wrong. The situation should worsen, to create tension. If Kalos becomes infected with an empathy virus, he could react in several ways. His character will determine whether he cries, commits suicide, denies his situation, seeks a cure, or uses his new power of empathy to reach out to others. So long as he doesn't just sit there, it's up to you what he does and his actions will create the plot.

> The progressive worsening of a problem makes a plot interesting.

Each problem your character faces should be worse than the last. If Kalos tries to fight the empathy drug, the next stage of the story should show the effects worsening.

As plot progresses, although the same problem will worsen, try not to repeat the problem in exactly the same way. If Kalos fights the effects with meditation, and then they worsen, he should fight them with self-mutilation rituals, a different drug, or by seeking violent confrontation. At this point you could increase the effects of the drug, to progress the plot. To make it really interesting there should be an additional threat. Kalos could risk losing his honour, a position in society, his job as a security herder, if he becomes too empathic. He could also lose his friends. By making the threat more painful, the plot worsens, and he will be forced to change to resolve the problem.

This aspect of plotting is especially important in science fiction, because it re-emphasises your core idea in a logical way.

Applying logic

When you work creatively you may think that logic is anathema to your process, but it shouldn't be. Although the world is often illogical, and our actions don't make sense, fiction works best when plots evolve logically. Avoid over-use of coincidence, chance happenings and out-of-character events. If you stick to the logic of your characters, theme, situation and idea, the plot will evolve in an impressive way.

● In science fiction, fantasy and horror you must maintain a strict logic, in keeping with your world-building.

If curse spells don't work in crystal caves, then your character must find another way to hold back the Orcs. If Angramar Wolves drink fresh river water, you won't find them in cities. If warp drives can't be used near worm holes on page 20, then you can't warp away from a worm hole on page 60. When plotting, the restrictions of the logical world you create will help, rather than hinder, because they urge you to find credible, interesting solutions rather than obvious, less exciting ideas.

Letting characters develop

The change that occurs in your character is the most important part of a story. Plot can show how this change comes about. If this story is about Kalos' lack of self respect, and the way he must change this, then we must see the change in him. The story could be resolved when he accepts the empathy effects and, through a new self respect, allows himself to be close to others.

A plot should progress to the worst possible moment, at which point the story should be resolved through the actions of your character. It may be resolved positively, with your character's change and actions achieving the desired result, or it may end in tragedy. Whatever ending you choose, it should be brought about by character *action*.

The worst mistake you can make is to show somebody thinking, 'I know what to do.' *Show* us what they do. Never tell us what a character has decided. Show us through action. If Kalos decides that he can form new relationships, don't let him mull this over; show him transmatting over to his brother's house, offering the hand of reconciliation.

When editors say a story needs a stronger plot, this is what they mean. They aren't asking for more action in terms of battles and explosions, they are asking for a story built around a situation. They want you to develop your character in response to a conflict, so that as the character changes the story can be resolved.

FORMING A SUBPLOT

Subplots occur in almost all films, most novels and many short stories. They are secondary stories, plots that run alongside the main plot. If the main story is about one character's fight against a disease, the subplot could concern his partner's battle to tell him a difficult truth before he dies.

Connecting plot with subplot

Plot and subplot should be closely linked. If you think of your main plot as a river, flowing progressively on, the subplots can be thought of as the streams that feed it. They should not be arbitrary, but should be tied up with the matters of the main plot.

Subplots give novels broader scope, but the downside is that they also make a novel less focused. Use subplots carefully, to enhance a story, rather than simply to add extra action.

CLOSING A PLOT

In desperation for a good ending it is often tempting to bring in a *deus ex machina* – where some outside event solves the problems. This was recently used in the film *Jurassic Park*. The characters are put into a really dreadful situation at the end, with dinosaurs approaching from all sides. The film makers chose to solve this by having a bigger dinosaur crash through the building, by coincidence.

No matter how impressive the special effects, most of the audience was disappointed by this, because it had nothing to do with the people we had been watching for two hours. It happened by chance and, as such, meant nothing. We wanted to see the characters resolve a situation. *Jurassic Park* should have been about people fighting dinosaurs, not about chance happenings.

In your own fiction maintain the integrity of the story, and give it the most relevant and logical ending. There is no such thing as a good ending, only the *right* ending for your story.

CHECKLIST

● Analyse plots of your favourite stories and novels.

● Look at the logic of your idea.

● Examine cause and effect in fiction.

● Notice how plot worsens.

● Imagine the full scope of your story.

● Ensure that your plot arises from the character's situation.

● Develop a plot that tests your main character.

● Let the conflict develop, becoming progressively more difficult.

● Allow character to develop within the events of your plot.

● Study subplot in fiction that you enjoy.

● Make room for subplot, to add depth to your story.

● Find the right ending for your story.

CASE STUDIES

Peter evolves a plot

While writing scenes of interaction, Peter realises that Brian's misguided actions will have negative consequences. He writes the first part of the story, showing that once the brain valve is in place it stops the memories. A side effect is that Brian's piano playing is now passionless, meaning he is liked even less. Peter now makes notes on the way this plot can evolve. These are general notes, showing a meeting with the friend, another meeting with the surgeon and the realisation that resolving this contradiction will be his purpose in the story. With that basic plan Peter continues to write, letting the scenes and plot evolve as he writes.

Michael increases the conflict

To give direction to his plot Michael imagines several different endings. He is still uncertain exactly how the story will end, but he determines a general direction and begins writing. To make the plot more effective, he makes sure that the events of the story progress, with the conflict becoming more severe. He realises that to make the story work he has to write scenes of action which show Liam's suffering and conflict. In each case the problem gets worse, gradually forcing Liam to change.

Ruth expands her story

Ruth finds that to make her story effective, the discoveries about Elissa must come quite early in the story. At first she thought that this revelation would be the conclusion to the plot, but now believes it is the starting point for development. While writing the story she finds that, although the professor only sees skin deep, he has a depth of character which she wants to bring out in him. As she writes scenes of interaction between him and Elissa he is forced to face up to her true character, and thus forced to see her as a person. The plot resolves only when he has changed, using his invention as a form of communication rather than control.

DISCUSSION POINTS

1. As your story develops, examine the plot. Is it getting progressively worse? Does the conflict test your character's weakness?

2. Imagine different endings for your story. Which is the most interesting? Which will demand the most of the character? Which ending helps to make sense of your theme and ideas?

3. Characters must develop, in order to resolve a plot. How can your character change, to make the story work?

4. Subplot works best when it reflects the main plot. How can you build a subplot around the main events of your story?

6
Making Your Story Believable

CREATING REALISM

Science fiction should be believable. No matter how fantastic your ideas, images, or aliens, your reader should believe that your fictional world is realistic. Thankfully, readers do suspend disbelief, even with wondrous stories, but they will only go so far. If you write an implausible scene, an out of character action, or a poor sentence, readers will notice. When they notice a mistake, suspension of disbelief evaporates and your work is ruined.

To make readers believe your story you need to write realistically, giving everything reason, focus and meaning.

WRITING REALISTICALLY

To make fiction realistic you need a realistic character. The work you did earlier on defining a character will ensure that your viewpoint is a realistic one. If your main character acts within the boundaries of a recognised personality, your story should be believable.

Characters will develop and change, thus altering their characteristics, but this will happen in a reasonable way. Some shifts will be gradual, others will be sudden, but they should always be logical. A cowardly character, for example, may suddenly find the courage to enter a rat-infested Combat Tunnel. That would make sense if his son was trapped at the other end, screaming for help. If nobody was trapped, and he was doing it for the laugh, it would seem artificial. The transformation wouldn't ring true. After you have written a scene, ask yourself whether or not it rings true for your character.

Realising the unreal

In SF you have the additional problem of describing aliens, spaceships and technology that simply doesn't exist. How can you make something unreal realistic?

Again, using a strong character can solve many problems. Imagine your character's perspective on events and show that. If she lives in a futuristic landscape crusted with light towers, transfer beams and shipping floaters, then these things may not be wondrous to her. They should be described in a matter of fact way. If, however, the towers have just been built, and she is seeing them for the first time, they will have a great impact on her. Before writing any scene of wonder, think of the character's viewpoint.

Giving a sense of wonder

Your reader will still feel a sense of wonder when reading about advanced technological ideas, even if the character takes them for granted. This technique can even increase the sense of wonder; when something so unusual is taken for granted it seems an even greater achievement. In this decade we take home computers for granted, but just 20 years ago the concept was almost alien. If the people of the 1960s saw a vision of tiny, super-powerful home computers being taken for granted, that would seem wondrous.

Grounding a story

The most difficult aspect of SF is describing an imagined future, while making it something that contemporary readers can relate to. This is easier with near-future SF, where the world is only slightly different. In a far future, or on a different planet, the task is much greater because life as we know it may have been completely eradicated.

Drawing on today's concerns

To make a story meaningful, and believable, you should ground it in a contemporary concern. Science fiction is concerned with the future, but these speculations are important to us because they reflect the world today. A story about emotion-drugs is important, not because of the science but because it reflects modern-day use of alcohol and illegal drugs. An epic on the subject of Terraforming Mars matters to us now, because it reflects current environmental concerns.

No matter how mythological a scientific development may

appear, it soon becomes mundane. A story about video games, cars, aeroplanes, or telephones would be boring, not only because the technology is familiar but because it is the way these creations affect humans that matters. In the same way stories about virtual reality, teleportation and space travel are also boring, unless they do more than show the obvious implications of the technology. Always remember the human angle.

> SF questions our achievements, hints at our responsibilities, asks where we are going and who we are today.

Whatever your idea and theme, and no matter how abstract, consider these factors to ensure that your story matters. If you can make readers care, they will want to believe.

Revealing your 'world view'
In SF, fantasy and horror you have to establish the unique world you are writing about, within a few lines. If your story is set three hundred years from now, you should make that clear as soon as possible to avoid reader confusion.

If your first scene describes a man meeting somebody else in a park, and shows them talking, you should try to make it clear what era the story is set in. Otherwise readers may feel that it is set in the present day, and when the characters teleport up to the moon the story will lack realism.

To establish the date (without stating it directly), build details of the future into the opening scene. You could show them smoking self-lighting cigarettes which give off a blue smoke, while gazing across at the sky tower which winds all the way into space.

When the strange and new is taken for granted in a story it will seem more believable, yet more wondrous. If we were to show somebody from four hundred years ago Tower Bridge in London, they would be amazed, even though we take it for granted. Your characters should be equally unabashed by modern technologies.

Taking technology for granted
Avoid over-explaining. If you must explain how something works, such as a hover car, try to do so with relevance. One way around this is to show it being something that concerns the character. With this example you could say:

'As the car lifted off, Jed hoped the tetrion-coil had been replaced recently. It wasn't that he didn't like fly-cars, just that he would rather go by a ground-rail.'

These brief sentences take the technology for granted, which makes it realistic yet also show us how the machinery works. At the same time this also reveals a little bit about Jed's techno-phobic character.

When writing a novel set in the present we don't describe how a combustion engine works, how Tower Bridge was built, the principles of flight and so on. In SF technology is integral, but it isn't all about explaining.

● Ensure that your story is internally logical, believable, and that everything is relevant.

By all means spend half a page describing the twin suns over the coal mountains – if the story requires it, if the mood is necessary – but don't ramble for the sake of it. Too much SF is glossy on the surface, without intelligent content, so write with integrity. Every word should contribute towards the whole of the piece.

Your fiction should do more than simply report on the future; it should comment on human nature, helping us to stand back and observe ourselves in the moment of now.

Accepting the unusual

A character should not get too involved with the technology, unless the technology is changing for the character. Although a transportation pad might be unusual to us, if it is ordinary for your character he should not show too much shock about seeing one outside his house. A contemporary story would not say 'Conrad turned on the television, a glass and plastic device used for viewing coded information signals, relayed by an electron beam, as images, resembling a two-dimensional version of a framed reality.' You would just say that he watched TV. In the same way, if you over-explain it becomes obvious that you are writing down to the character.

The skill is to use assumptions in a way that does reveal information. There are two main approaches to revealing world view:

- the first is subtle and gradual
- the second is more direct.

Revealing information gradually
In the first approach you will describe a character who is recognisable to us in terms of habits, preferences and desires (even if this person is an alien). The unusual aspects of the imagined world will be revealed gradually, through the first few scenes. Rather than stating that Earth was run by an organic computer, which provided nutrients to the people in State Supply Tubes on street corners, you would be more subtle. Your first scene could involve characters sitting in a café, drinking only water, feeling hungry, but unable to order food. As they talk it becomes obvious that this isn't our world. When they are too hungry to continue talking they could, mater of factly, go out to the State Buffet Slabs, pull out a sugar tube, and ingest. At this point one character might say it's time for his hibernation.

Bombarding information
The other extreme goes straight for the science fiction.

> 'There were full moons in the sky when the Kramma ships finally arrived. Ingmar watched from the his sailbarge, as the ships unfolded their wings.'

This style has the advantage of instantly creating a strong impression of your imagined world. Its main disadvantage is that you may lose readers if your ideas are too extreme. If you do bombard information, do so in certain sections, but use a more gradual style elsewhere so that readers have time to adjust to the ideas.

ENCOUNTERING ALIENS

Aliens, by definition, are unusual to us. Even if your character has mixed with aliens for years, they will still feel non-human. To make aliens interesting, however, we must be able to relate to them. Humanoid aliens, with distorted foreheads, double noses or eyes in their cheeks, are easier to cope with than slime spheres or conscious gases.

Many writers go for the easy option, using only humanoid aliens. This is the greatest weakness of television series such as *Star*

Trek. After a while the aliens all come to seem a little too human, too recognisable. Humanoid aliens are difficult to justify in scientific terms, and although they are easy to relate to they may seem more unrealistic than non-humanoids.

Concentrating on character

If you do write about slime globes or similar, non-humanoid aliens, you can still make them realistic. Again, think of your character's perception.

● Just because an alien is weird doesn't mean it is unrealistic.

If you describe a slime sphere well, with a fully imagined home planet, history, means of communication and social organisation, it will be believable. Make sure that you appreciate what type of air it breathes, what it eats, how long it lives for, what religion it may have and so on.

Making the anatomy believable

In terms of anatomy, make sure that everything is there for a reason. Don't give a monster tentacles to make it more dramatic. If it has tentacles they should be present for a reason: does it use them to catch humming flies, to mate with, as weapons, sensory organs, or even for communication?

This is why imagining a home world for aliens is vital. Even if it is never described in your story it makes the appearance of your aliens logical and sensible.

HANDLING TIME

All fiction deals with imagined moments of life. Instead of writing down a character's entire existence, from birth through to death, chronicling every meal, day-dream and accident, detail scenes which are relevant to your story. Fiction is a way of packaging life and looking at the interesting bits. In SF, fantasy and horror getting the pace of a story right is a vital aspect of making it believable.

Sometimes you describe every moment of a scene, detailing the exact sensation and observation. At other times you describe decades in a sentence. Most of the time you will work in the middle-ground, making the transition between scenes as smooth as possible. To the reader it shouldn't be obvious that you are playing with time, only that you are concentrating on the most important parts of the story.

If, for example, two characters go out for a meal, the events before and after they eat may be relevant. To avoid a boring description of the meal itself, you could write:

'She smiled as she took the first mouthful, already feeling the heat. By the end of the meal she was too hot, finding it difficult to breathe. Perhaps the implant was playing up.'

Here time is speeded up, then slowed down again, smoothly.

Making larger shifts

In SF, more than any other type of fiction, you will often be required to make large time shifts. These can be anything from one to a hundred million years. When you describe large segments of time you have to judge the degree of required detail. 'For the next decade he worked alone' might be sufficient. 'By the end of the century, the first solar mills were in place' might work in some stories, but in others much more detail will be required. Although massive shifts in time can be handled in a moment, you may want to spend several pages describing the century, and exactly what happened, both in the world and to your character.

Large-scale time transitions are quite difficult, though, because they can be impersonal, so pepper them with scenes where possible.

'After three years without seeing Lallan, he met her in a Kimota bar. They barely spoke. She was wearing too much skull makeup, and looked drowsy. He thought about that for weeks afterwards, while working at the Freezer, but by the time they met again, during Middlemas season, he'd forgotten what she looked like.'

Pacing a story may seem complicated, but it is simple if you follow one rule:

● only include the relevant information, or to put it another way, give everything a reason.

Giving everything a reason

If a scene, explanation, description or conversation doesn't contribute in some way to the overall story, it shouldn't be there. So if time is passing in your story, with years going by, ask yourself whether a description of the intervening events really is essential. If not, simply state that the years have gone by. If detail is needed, decide how much. Sometimes pages or chapters will be required, in other cases a paragraph will suffice.

When writing creatively you shouldn't question yourself too much, or you will stem the flow of words. Once a scene, description, or passage of time has been written, however, ask yourself if it really belongs in the story. Does it have a reason to be there? Determine whether the passage:

- moves the story forward
- reveals character
- establishes mood and atmosphere
- expresses the theme.

If it does at least one of these, then it probably belongs in your work. If it doesn't do any of these, it is unnecessary padding that will make your story sluggish, so you might want to cut it out. Equally, if a scene restates something the readers already know, drop it. If you show two characters arguing about compassion on page three, it would be boring to see them arguing about it again on page seven. It could be interesting if the argument has changed in meaning or intensity, implying change in the characters, or significance in relation to events. Otherwise, every line should offer something new.

USING MISTAKES AS INSPIRATION

As you write the story, with new elements being introduced and developed, check to see that your world view still holds together. If there are contradictions, arising from new ideas, readers will notice.

Look for loopholes in the plot, by asking yourself if there is an easier way out of a situation. If, for example, your main character is trapped on a planet, trying to steal a shuttle so that he can escape, this might not make sense if his mother-ship has tele-portation capability. In this example you will either have to disable the teleportation through an accident of some kind, or remove the ship from this location, or make his signal impossible to receive.

In some way you must maintain the logic, without it looking as though you are forcing the facts to suit your situation.

Use these discrepancies to add interest and excitement. If you regard them as opportunities, they can bring new ideas to your work.

CHECKLIST

● Is your character suited to the story?

● Are your character's actions believable?

● Make readers care about a character, to help them believe in your story.

● Use assumptions, rather than explanation, to reveal technology.

● Imagine the full consequences of every action in your story.

● Reveal your world view through revelation and bombardment.

● Check that every line genuinely contributes to the story.

● Find loopholes in your plot and use them to develop your work.

CASE STUDIES

Peter works on world building

With the story now complete, Peter checks on the logic of his idea. He realises that the idea of just one surgeon having this capability is a little implausible. This makes him develop a culture in which there is an entire black market of such brain valves. He now makes more notes, building a fuller picture of his world. Rewriting the story the surgeon now takes on a more sinister appearance, and Brian's actions feel more daring, giving a greater level of realism.

Michael works with character

Michael works on world building, to ensure that the Loneliness

Hour has a logical cause. This, in turn, affects other aspects of the story, which require development. To give cohesion to this rewriting process, Michael concentrates on Liam's character. By making him a character that readers will sympathise with, the story is more believable. In the first section Michael uses idea bombardment to set the scene, later revealing information gradually, so that the ideas are revealed within the story rather than as explanations.

Ruth reveals information
Looking back over her story Ruth realises that its steady tone, and formal setting, mean that it will be suited to a calm style, with gradual revelations. Using scenes of argument and action, she reveals her imagined world, without explaining. The important information is set out immediately, with more detail being released throughout the story.

DISCUSSION POINTS

1. Take a scene from your story and write it using gradual revelations. Now rewrite it using bombardment. Which is most effective? How can you combine the two?

2. Look for mistakes in your work. What areas of development do they suggest?

3. Examine the events that are occurring in your story. Does everything have a reason?

4. Read the first page of your story. How quickly do you establish your world view? Have you left room for the development of this idea?

7
Bringing Science Fiction to Life

Science fiction, fantasy and horror are renowned for rich imagery, stunning scenes and a sense of wonder. When used well your descriptive language can convey images, sensory impressions, emotion and atmosphere. Precise, imaginative description is an area of huge potential and is neglected by many writers. If you learn to create strong imagery, your stories can be more complete.

CREATING IMAGERY

One of the most effective ways to create a striking visual effect is through juxtaposition.

> 'Embarrassed, she moved towards one of the plastic tables, placing her daffodil beside a runny sauce bottle.'

By placing something fragile and beautiful next to something mundane, each object is given more visual impact and a specific atmosphere is created.

You can experiment with such visual techniques in note-form, to get the feel for the process, before actually writing them into a story or a novel. When you come to write fiction let the description occur naturally, as a part of the writing process. Never describe for the sake of it; use the description when the story would be flat without it, when the story requires that the reader be aware of more than is already implied by the situation or dialogue.

Calming your style

Maintain a steady writing style, and avoid too many adjectives and adverbs. The worst mistake a writer can make when describing is to over-do it. Over-writing is a major problem in any area of fiction, and it makes descriptions sound ridiculous. Not only are 'towering mountains' and 'sparkling stars' clichés, but they are ruined by adjectives. It is often enough to point out that the stars were out and that the character observed them.

It is possible to describe a rich scene without adjectives. Sometimes, simply cutting the adjectives will strengthen a piece.

Going beyond the obvious

In science fiction these slightly altered ways of looking at things are also an essential part of describing an imaginary world. If your story is set in the far future, you can't use similes and adjectives in the same way. If apples no longer exist, for example, you couldn't compare an alien's skin to the flesh of an apple. Nor could you say that a rocket engine glowed with the colour of a street light. Going beyond the obvious, and using more original descriptions, is the best way around this problem.

If you describe a sunset, the obvious description will concern the clouds, the sun and the colour of the sky. It is more interesting to describe the effect of the sunset on the surrounding land. Imagine, for example, sunset light on someone's face, or sunset brightening the landscape beneath thickening clouds.

> Don't look straight into the obvious glare of an image. Look to one side, see how it affects *people*.

When the sun sets most people stare straight at it, and are blind to whatever it illuminates. By looking in a new way, observing things other than the obvious, you can uncover original descriptions. If you are describing mountains, it's more important to show the character's perception of them than to convey their factual appearance.

Revealing perception

Perception is the whole point of description. The way a character perceives snow, for instance, says more about *them* than it does about the scenery. A sad character will be aware of the cloying, wet effects of the stuff, as it finds its way into nostrils and ears. A happy character will kick the snow playfully, or enjoy the numbing freeze working through her boots.

● When describing, always remember that you are conveying the *character*'s perception.

This is the purpose of writing: to convey levels of meaning and emotions which lie in the subtle space between labels such as happy and sad.

Describing original images

There is always a new way to describe something, no matter how often it has been observed by another. Your own perception will always be original, so don't be afraid of sunsets, mountains or snow. You can make them your own, by writing with honest perception. Snow, for instance, is difficult to describe in an original way. If you observe it carefully you could say that some flakes move faster than others, and that against the sky they look grey. The problem here is that this is too direct and analytical. If you imagine a character perceiving the snow it can be seen in a new way.

When you simply look at flakes, they are nothing other than shapes and shades. When somebody stands in a snow storm as part of your fiction, snow can compete with tears on the cheeks, or breath in the mouth. In this way description isn't only a way of expressing your story, it is a way of finding out what is happening to your characters. Look at the way your characters see the world, and you will understand them better.

SHOWING EMOTION THROUGH IMAGERY

> The beauty of fiction is that it allows you to express a whole range of emotions, which we are unable to name.

By integrating imagery into a story, it reveals emotions without you having to make statements about how the characters feel.

Integrating imagery

Without description fiction is only a collection of ideas. Images enable you to communicate exact moods and emotions, whether you write hard SF or violent horror. Description brings fiction to life, but it often falls into cliché and can be over-used. To avoid this use description as an integral part of the writing process, rather than as something that is tagged on for effect.

To make a scene work well, mingle:

- character thought
- observation
- action.

'The light wasn't strong enough to warm her arms, but Derian could hear the Lake Cleansers powering up, triggered by dawn. Promising herself this was the last sabotage she'd help Avery with, she edged up to the closest boulder, and saw the Cleansers waddle out of their Kevlar nest. Their legs were squat like a lizard's, moving silently, smelling like burnt paper. She could make out the wood-coloured veins running through their shells, with shadows like needles flickering in the core. As the first one skulked under the surface, leaving a slap of ripples, she unclipped her grenade.'

The writer hasn't broken off to 'do some description'. As well as describing, we are clearly moving through the events of the story, and thoughts of the character. This is more effective than stating what happened, what she saw, what she thought. By mingling the events, as an experience, it is much more realistic.

When description is used in this way, the sensations are part of the central character's experience. Description should be the relevant experience of your main character.

Creating description without images

Description is more than imagery. Many writers never get beyond describing the most basic visual icons, while neglecting the other senses. Thinking visually and picturing scenes is useful, but appreciate all senses, noting how they can be relevant to your writing.

The following extract is highly descriptive, and gives the reader a strong impression of the scene, without any visual references as such.

'On my way out of Catherine's flat that night she got me, draped her arms about my neck like a damp scarf and pouted for a kiss.'

The description is based around the way the narrator feels about Catherine, the way she appears to him. There is no record of what her lips or arms actually look like, but this description conveys how she appeared to him. This allows the reader to imprint their own visuals on a situation.

This technique is especially effective when combined with assumed technologies, as described in Chapter 6.

'I stroked her hair, my fingers hesitating over the lip of her external drive on the back of her neck. It was empty.'

This sounds unusual to us, but because the character takes it for granted we believe it. The mention of a lip makes this visual enough, without a full description of the exact appearance.

When you write about technology which is bizarre to the reader, but mundane to the character, it is wise to describe without much detail.

USING THE SENSES TO REVEAL MOOD

Perception, by definition, relies on our senses. This is why describing specific sensations gives a good impression of reality. Rather than saying 'it was hot' describe the heat on a particular part of the body. Heat felt in the head is different to burning sun on your arms.

Your story should make use of all the senses.

Describing sound

Express the sounds of your story. We all know how important the sound of dialogue is – whether imposed through description of the voice, or by the choice of words – but many writers neglect sound in the story itself. You don't even need to use description in the mode of metaphor or simile; simply mentioning a phone going off, or a window breaking, if used carefully, can create the correct mood. There are ways, however, of describing sounds in new ways, to create surprising effects. 'She dipped her spoon into her cup, sucked it, then clattered it on her teeth.'

Using taste sensations sparingly

Taste is also important, but should be used sparingly. Don't waste time describing the tangy bite of a cup of coffee, unless it reflects something that is happening to the character. The copper taste of a nose bleed, however, could be highly relevant to a scene.

Suggesting reality through touch

The sense of touch is so underestimated that many writers hardly ever use it. This is perhaps because making touch relevant or original is difficult. When it works, though, touch adds an impression of reality that few of the other senses can match. 'When I woke up it was because clouds had covered the sun and great splatters of rain were falling on my bare arms.'

Remembering through smell

Smell should never be underestimated, as it cuts straight to the emotional memory of the reader. It is impossible to read the following quote without feeling the atmosphere of the room described:

> 'The cellar smelled of old books, dirty water and plants, but as she went further it gave way to an odour of mould and peaches.'

Use the senses exactly, because they are a direct source of realism and help to establish emotion and atmosphere.

CHECKLIST

- To describe effectivity, observe accurately.

- Use all five senses.

- Describe the specific perceptions of sensations.

- Use juxtaposition to make a strong point.

- Avoid using clichés and adjectives.

- Go beyond the obvious when describing.

- Be wary of using contemporary metaphors for stories set in the future.

- Use the character's perception of sensation, to reveal emotion.

- Describe without imagery, to make technology appear ordinary.

CASE STUDIES

Peter goes beyond the obvious
Peter's story is based entirely on Brian's perceptions and mis-perceptions, so it is important for him to make his description effective. In some scenes he makes it clear that Brian feels oppressed by his 'friends', although the reader can see that they are trying to be helpful. Once the brain valve has been fitted Peter blunts Brian's perceptions, reflecting the damping effect it has on his emotions. Working in this way, Peter ties Brian's emotional state to the description and imagery.

Michael works with character
Michael has written lots of descriptive scenes, but these all spoil the flow of the story. He rewrites these scenes, building the descriptions into character action. He enhances his description by looking at the way his character perceives sensations in relation to his mood. During the scenes of the Loneliness Hour, Liam's perception darkens, so that everything is seen from a bleak and hopeless perspective. To make these descriptions more powerful Michael builds in extra observations of smell and touch.

Ruth reveals information
The weakest areas of Ruth's story concern the professor's percep-tion of Elissa. Although he is only meant to be observing her at a surface level, Ruth finds that the observations are littered with clichés. To get around this problem she shows the professor observing Elissa doing specific things, in specific situations. By describing the way Elissa acts, rather than just how she appears, the descriptions become more effective. Ruth builds on the images and emotions set out in her first draft, by contrasting the sleepy Oxford atmosphere with the shock of new technologies.

DISCUSSION POINTS

1. Look over your story for the sections of description. Is this description built into the actions, or is it separate? How can you integrate the two?

2. Take a scene of description from your story. Rewrite it, ensuring that you use the character's mood and emotions to reflect perception.

3. Write about the science fiction elements of your story, without imagery, as though taking them for granted. Does this make them seem more realistic?

4. Find examples of all five senses in your story. Which sense is used most? Which is used the least? How can you restore the balance?

8
Developing Your Style

Style is the sound of a writer's 'voice' and yours should be unique. When used well style can enhance mood and emotions, through dialogue and description. SF, fantasy and horror writers are often remembered for their style as much as their stories, so it's worth working on your own way.

Style is concerned with the way that you write, as much as with what you write about. The following examples show a variety of styles, each saying roughly the same thing:

- 'Paula darkened the windows a little, then pulled the slider right down, blacking out the sunset.'

- 'She darkened the windows, slammed the slider and blacked out the view.'

- 'Paula dozed the scenery out, first to haze, then tar-flicked it.'

- 'The sunset browned as she faded her window, buildings and clouds becoming black outlines. Her fingers hesitated on the controls, but then she pulled the slider down, quick as a blink, and the scenery was gone, replaced with blackness and her own reflection.'

None of these is necessarily better than any other, but some are easier to read and all have different effects. As the latter example shows, the length of a piece also affects style. In a short story you have less room for manoeuvre, so a tighter, more compact style is required.

SETTING THE TONE

The style you choose to work in should arise from the overall tone of the story you are creating. It may be similar to one of the above styles, or it may be something totally new. There could be many other versions, determined by the subject and characters being written about.

Often the nature of the character, era, planet, society, the mood and the setting will dictate a story's tone. A story set in a cybertech future, with frantic drug taking, will have a hip, rapid, illusory, slang-ridden style. A story set in a quasi-Utopian society is more likely to have a more subtle, perhaps Miserablist tone.

Juxtaposition can be impressive, if you clash a style of writing with the culture. A 'street' style of writing, set in a romantic age, could work, but only if this clash also existed within the story.

Style isn't usually something that becomes apparent when note-taking. Once you begin writing, however, you will find your story settling into a tone, approach and feel.

● Check that the tone of your story suits its mood and aims.

Imagine that you have never read the story and feel the type of atmosphere it creates.

Altering the mood through style

Style can be used as a technique, to create specific effects. If, for instance, you want to create excitement, you can use short, sharp sentences. This doesn't mean every sentence should consist of a few staccato words, but that a more urgent tone will create an urgent atmosphere.

'The windscreen wipers froze, the screen matting with rain. He didn't feel an impact, but the windscreen flew out like powder. Salty rain covered his hands, stinging.'

Be wary of overkill, though, because too many short sentences can be frustrating for readers and soon becomes an obvious device. An alternative is to use long sentences, which convey lots of action, from the viewpoint of a bewildered character. This sense of calm during panic is realistic, and can be chilling.

Excitement is also generated through suspense, where there is the promise of something happening.

'Storms were forecast, but the sky was featureless white. That was a relief, because he didn't want to put his face-tank on. It only held an hour's worth of air, and the last inhabited village was more than an hour behind. The next one might be as far again. If it came to that, the tank would only put off the suffocation, no matter how fast he drove.'

Here, the style reflects the events, with hints and suggestions, matching the actual suspense and fear experienced by the character.

Styling for horror
In horror an understated, matter of fact style can be the most oppressive and frightening.

'The sunshine made my hangover thump, and the berries on the rowan tree seemed to pulse. I drew a branch towards me, trying to focus. Each berry darkened, then went light, throbbing in time with my headache. I held one fruit between my fingers, and as I pressed felt the crackling of tiny bones. Something red went down my arm.'

Style is just as important during solemn and steady moments as it is during times of excitement, shock and wonder, so pay attention to style at all times.

Controlling your style
Over-writing can occur with any word, if it is forced into a sentence. 'He cramped himself into the front of the shuttle' may actually be relevant, if the shuttle is small and the character is large, but if not this is over-writing.

'She skipped down the street' may express happiness, but it is probably going too far. 'Stephen slumped into the dwell-sac' could be good writing if he really is tired, otherwise it's over-writing.

It is the *context* of these words that makes a style meaningful.

● Check through your work, to see if it is over-written.

- It is also possible, although less likely, that you could be under-writing.

If every sentence is completely straightforward, it will tend to sound as though you are saying 'She did this, then this happened and then this.' Under-written stories can sound boring, lacking a narrative drive that compels the reader to read on. Enrich your style, to suit the mood of your fiction. Use style as a writing tool, a means of expression, rather than the whole point of your story, and it will improve everything that you write.

BEING SPECIFIC

An effective way to improve your style, while enhancing the impact of a story, is to use specific words rather than generalisations. When describing a scene you will tend to say 'trees' instead of 'sycamores', or 'fruit' instead of 'apples'. In most cases more specificity will improve a description.

'At the next street he went down steps to the level of the river. Looking across to the stone banks at the cathedral, green with plants, he tried to make out the place where he met Ameline.'

This simple line can be made more specific, by changing a few general words.

'At Pont De Sully he went down steps to the level of the Seine. Looking across to the walled banks at Notre Dame, green with ivy, he tried to make out the bench where he met Ameline.' This expresses more, without becoming wordy.

Being specific is one of the most efficient writing techniques, and can be built into all your work. It is an instant way of adding an impression of description, without actually describing. If you build this specific word selection into your writing it will improve your style by enriching your language.

Adding motifs

Many writers enhance the style of a story, by building **motifs** into the work. Motifs are words, phrases or images which are repeated throughout a story to create a specific effect.

It is the repetition of a story element that makes it a motif, and thus adds to its significance. If your story involves a character seeing an injured bird, that is simply an image. If your character also dreams about injured birds, or sees several injured birds during the story, it becomes a significant motif.

Using motifs effectively
As the above example shows, motifs can stretch credibility because they rely on coincidence to an extent. When used subtly, however, they can work well.

Motifs should reflect an idea or theme, occurring at specific points in the story, rather than arbitrarily. The injured bird motif could work in a story concerned with compassion. The motif could appear every time the character has to face loss of some kind. The way the character reacts to the motif would change and thus be significant.

This technique works, even if the motif is so subtle that readers don't notice it consciously. If you mention a light bulb blowing, during two violent scenes, this won't necessarily seem significant. If you then write a calm scene in which a light bulb blows, this will set up a tension in the reader, preparing them for more violence.

You will find that motifs occur of their own accord as you write.

CHECKLIST

● Avoid over-long sentences.

● Use short sentences sparingly, to create tension and excitement.

● Apply style technique to every line of your whole story.

● Use motifs carefully, to reflect your theme.

● Alter the style through word choice.

● Let style reflect the events and emotions of your story.

● Be specific when describing.

● Cut sentences which are over-written.

● Ensure that your style is relevant to the story.

CASE STUDIES

Peter adjusts his style

Peter looks back over his story and finds that towards the end it settles into a steady, yet harsh, style. This is the part of the story that works best, so he applies the same style throughout. Some scenes have to be changed slightly as a result, but he finds that overall the story is improved. By using specific words, instead of generalisations, he is able to cut some lengthy descriptions while retaining a sense of description.

Michael works with character

Michael's scenes of description have already been improved, but he improves the whole story by using specific observations throughout. He finds that the motif of watches occurs several times, perhaps reflecting the idea of the Loneliness Hour. He alters the story, so that the motif of the watch represents fear. This is particularly effective during a scene in which Liam awakens during the night, staring at the glow of his watch.

Ruth reveals information

Ruth checks through her text for over-writing and cuts accordingly. Although the story is now much tighter she feels that it is lacking in style. It reads well, but there is nothing unique about it. She takes one scene and rewrites it, experimenting with different styles. When she finds one that feels suitable, she rewrites the whole story.

DISCUSSION POINTS

1. Take a scene from your story and rewrite it in a different style. How does this alter its effectiveness?

2. Rewrite your story, turning general descriptions into specific observations. Why does this improve the story?

3. Read through some of your favourite stories. What motifs reoccur? How do they represent themes and ideas?

9
Dealing with Dialogue

When your characters speak they move the story forward and express emotion.

Creating realistic and effective dialogue will give your story an extra edge of reality.

CHOOSING A STYLE OF SPEECH

If you listen to people talking everybody has there own way of phrasing things. This *choice of words* is more important than the way they speak. In fact, choice of words can often imply a gruff tone, a quiet voice, or a stutter, without you having to mention it. In science fiction this will apply to all characters, whether they are androids, aliens or mutants.

Your primary task when writing dialogue is to give each character a recognisable way of speaking. In good fiction you should be able to tell who is speaking, without it being stated, through the choice of words. Although this sounds impossible to a beginner, you will find that well-imagined characters will generate their own voice.

All characters should use the correct language for their situation and background. A timid human will speak differently to a timid Wammak alien. Although an individual's characteristics will affect speech, in science fiction you should consider the nature of the character's race, culture and background.

Ordering words

The most subtle effects occur not through dialect, idiosyncratic phrases or expressions, but through the simple ordering and choice of words. We all do this naturally, when talking. The way you would ask somebody out for a meal would be radically different to the way your best friend would ask the same question. The choice of words, and the way in which they were spoken, would also vary, depending upon who you were asking out. This is why you should imagine a character speaking, to make sure that you don't simply put your own voice into every character's mouth.

Modifying speech

A character's style of speech will be determined by that person's overall nature, but will also be influenced by:

- who the character is speaking to
- how well they know each other
- the environment they are in
- the nature of the conversation
- the emotions present.

Using the way people speak

The *way* characters speak can tell us as much about them as *what* they say. A mumbling, stuttering character is clearly nervous, even if the actual words are forceful, as with 'Nothing's going to stop me.' To make this work you modify the sentence by adding 'he stuttered.'

Modifiers can ruin a good piece of writing, when over-used. In every page of dialogue you should have no more than a couple of modifiers. If every line contains something like 'he mumbled, she scolded, she replied, he snapped', you are over-writing. Use no more than one or two modifiers. The rest of the time you can simply use 'said'. This isn't as noticeable as you may think and is less boring than repeated modifiers.

To avoid the problem altogether, you can build dialogue into action. 'Jane looked up, chewing a finger nail. "I don't know what to do." ' In this example you don't even need to say 'she said' because it is obvious that she is speaking.

Hearing the sounds

Try to imagine the sound of the character's voice, as you write. If it doesn't sound realistic, take it out. Let the characters speak for themselves. Imagine them, imagine what is about to happen, and in your mind hear how they talk. This sounds deceptively simple, but many writers believe it is the best way to test dialogue.

The difference between 'Did you hear about Stuart?' and 'I suppose you heard about Stuart?' might seem small, but could change the tone of a scene. Without the writer telling us how this was said, we can detect a different tone of voice for each. The meaning of the words is just about the same, but the way it applies to the scene is different.

The simplest way to get this right is to ask yourself, 'What would a person really say in this situation?' People don't make speeches, and they don't always sound good. Real people use poor expressions and mess things up when talking. If that suits the characters you are writing about, let them speak that way.

MAKING DIALOGUE REALISTIC

Read over the lines you have written and see if they sound realistic.

Avoid, 'As you know I must get back to the station, so I will leave.' People never make statements in this way and it is a poor way of revealing information. To a reader this dialogue is obviously created by a writer; it sounds unrealistic and it spoils a story.

To make the above example more realistic, your character could say, 'I'm off, I'll be back later.' Another character might say, 'I'm going now, love. See you later. All right?' The same meanings, but these are different in terms of characterisation and mood. These don't sound as though they are written; they sound like speech and each does more than reveal words. Both move the story forward, while revealing character and even relationship.

Developing a conversation

Used correctly, dialogue can contribute more than conversation to a story. The basic rule, as ever, is to choose your words carefully. Don't include every conversation, or every line of a particular conversation. Only use the conversations and lines that you need.

In many cases you can bypass whole scenes of dialogue, with something such as 'He continued to ramble on', or, 'She told me the whole story, as we flew over the minefield.'

Dropping clichés

People often speak in clichés, but this doesn't give you the excuse to write them. Where possible avoid clichéd dialogue, except where the use of cliché expresses character. A person who continually adds, 'know what I mean' to the end of every sentence is conveyed well by cliché, but readers don't want to read too many lines of 'well basically' or 'at the end of the day.' Clichés are irritating, so use them with care. Writers choose the words that give the best impression of a conversation, not an actual conversation, so it is good practice to drop clichés.

Imagine that your characters are real people, rather than stereotypes, and picture how they would speak. Although social background will influence a character, it is not the source of an entire personality. In science fiction class systems may be rife or abolished, or entirely different to ours. Other influences, such as religion, race, history, political allegiance and so on, could have more effect on speech. In almost all cases, though, your character's personality will have the strongest effect.

Conveying secrets

Dialogue is most effective when it reveals more than the character intends. In many cases the characters may not even realise what has been revealed. Only the reader can see the irony. If, for example, one character says 'I'm not certain where I'm going' this could mean two things. On the surface it means the character doesn't know her way home, but it could also reflect the character's mistakes in her personal life.

This type of irony should be used with caution, however, as it can smack of cleverness. Use it to add a layer of meaning, without being an obvious joke.

Another way to use this type of irony is to show contradiction. In real life people contradict themselves, especially in arguments. If you show a character saying 'I can never find enough time' it would be realistic to hear them say, 'There's nothing to do round here' a few lines later. People are full of contradictions, so use them to add realism and convey inner conflicts.

HANDLING THE LANGUAGE OF SCIENCE FICTION

Language evolves. The way we speak today is different to the way we spoke twenty years ago. New words are invented, such as internet, CD, along with phrases such as road rage and palimony, all reflecting developments in culture and technology.

We also evolve new styles of speech. When writing science fiction your speech should reflect an evolution in communication, while remaining readable. To do this you will have to invent new words which mirror the imagined world of your story.

Creating new words

For every new aspect of reality you imagine, you will need a new (but vaguely recognisable) word.

If you write about a teleportation system, think of a word or phrase that people would genuinely use to describe it. Today we say car instead of automobile, and TV instead of television, so a teleportation system could be known as a mat (from matter transference), or a porta.

Slang is realistic, so it is possible that a teleportation system would actually be known as a shifter or blaster.

● Consider who is talking, and whether they would use slang, ordinary terminology, or the technical name of an object.

Coping with translation

If your story contains an entirely alien race, you translate everything into English, apart from new words specific to their culture. When you write about aliens interacting with humans there is more of a problem.

You can pretend that a Universal Translator has been invented, but that may be stretching credibility too far. Another alternative is to set the story far into the future, when aliens and humans have learnt each other's language. If you are writing a first-contact story, however, you will have to deal with the learning of a new language. You don't have to invent an alien language, but in terms of plot you will have to allow time for an understanding to develop.

CHECKLIST

● Ensure that your dialogue reflects the character.

● Give each character a distinctive voice.

● Modify speech sparingly.

● Use action to show who is speaking.

● Adapt speech, according to the character's situation.

- Read out the lines, checking for realism.

- Cut unnecessary conversation.

- Drop clichés.

- Use irony and contradictory speech to reflect your theme.

- Invent new words and speech style, suitable for your story.

- Check for words which may be changed or replaced in the future.

CASE STUDIES

Peter rewrites the dialogue
When reading out the dialogue from his story Peter finds that much of it is unrealistic. The sentences are over-formed, sounding more like speeches than conversation. His characters are speaking *at* each other, rather than holding conversations. He rewrites the dialogue, imagining the people actually speaking, hearing the words they would use in his head. He finds that he has used the phrase 'brain valve' throughout the story, but realises that this is an archaic way of naming such a futuristic object. He writes down several technical names, such as Anachronistic Deviance Filter, along with the slang names Memlock and Wire, eventually opting for Blocker.

Michael cuts the modifiers
Michael's dialogue is quite effective in itself, but there are too many modifiers. Even after thorough revision, cutting most of them out, he finds that his speech contains the word 'said' too many times. By integrating speech with the actions of the characters he is able to cut these down. The dialogue in his story is much less jarring now, and each character has taken on a more distinctive voice.

Ruth reveals information
Ruth has deliberately used an old fashioned style of speech in her story, with occasional new words, to show the conflict in her society. Even so there are some phrases which aren't quite realistic,

so she cuts these out. In one section, where the professor is speaking to Elissa, Ruth builds in ironies and contradictions, to show the true situation.

DISCUSSION POINTS

1. Read the dialogue in your story out loud. Do any words sound unusual, or out of place? How can you make the speech more realistic?

2. Count the modifiers used in your story. Are they original? Are they all necessary? How can you avoid using too many?

3. Find a scene in which two people are speaking, and rewrite it without modifiers or clichés. Use action and style to make it clear who is speaking. Does this make the characters more distinctive?

4. Look for the science fiction aspects of your story, such as new technologies. Do their names sound plausible? Would they sound better if they were more like slang?

10
Rounding Off Your Work

CHOOSING HOW TO END

In the real world life goes on and there are no endings. In fiction endings round off your story and make it complete. When you put an ending on your story you are effectively saying, 'They may have lived happily ever after, but we are interested in what they did here.' It is a way of defining the scope of your story. Put simply, this principle sounds almost too obvious: the story ends when it has been told.

Endings are a vital part of a story, because they are all the reader is left with. The final paragraph and closing line seal your work. When timed correctly, and handled with care, a good ending does more than tie up loose ends. An ending should also:

● show how the character has changed
● reveal or restate the theme
● provide a last line or paragraph which represents the story.

In some stories the expected meaning of a story can be turned upside down. In others a particular image or event will restate the theme more powerfully.

A strong, relevant ending is especially important in SF, fantasy and horror because it is a way of fully defining an idea.

As well as making final points about your characters and theme, the ending will be a way of taking your idea to its limit.

Finding the right moment
An ending shouldn't be a dramatic moment, tagged on to a story. It should be the logical conclusion of all that has gone before. No

matter what the tone, pace, mood, theme or plot, the ending should come when the logical premise of your piece has been reached. Following the logic of plot you should reach a final moment, when the character must change to resolve the plot. Your character then fails or succeeds, and this dictates where the story will end. When written well this ending will also reflect the full expression of your idea and theme.

Making the ending logical
Whether you write a standard plotted story, based around cause and effect, or more experimental fiction, the ending should be logical. This doesn't mean it should be obvious, but it should be *fitting*.

Endings aren't necessarily dramatic, but they are significant, and involve more than thought or reflection. During the final page of your story something should happen which brings the plot to a conclusion. If the story is about trying to prevent an engine failure in a spaceship, it will end either when the problem is solved or when the engine blows up. You wouldn't end the story with gas streaming out of the matter conduits, with your hero about to take action. An ending always occurs after the character has taken the final, most difficult action of the story.

Winding down
Following this stage there is often a brief anti-climax, or wind down, where the story settles. This may consist of a few lines or a couple of paragraphs. This allows you to show:

● character reflection and understanding
● an appreciation of what has been achieved
● an impression of the story as a whole.

Knowing when to stop
Although you should avoid rambling on past the end of a story, *never end a story too soon*. If the character is facing problems, give them a fair chance to deal with these rather than closing before development has taken place. Endings can be left open, with nothing decided, or they may close on a negative note with everything going wrong. By choosing your moment of closure, you select the mood and attitude of the story.

When writing your final paragraphs, avoid summing up.

Although an ending should give an impression of summarising what has gone before, be wary of an ending that *only* summarises. The best endings offer a closing line that in some way sheds new light on the story.

The following approaches show some of the ways in which you can produce that last line.

Reflection and relevant observation
These summarise what has gone before by mood, rather than content, although the images may symbolise what has gone before.

Dialogue
Can stand alone or be combined with narration. ' "I won't be long," he said, knowing it was a lie.' Single lines, especially when repeating a phrase from earlier in the story, are extremely effective.

Memory
A memory can provide a powerful ending. If your main character remembers something of relevance this can add something new to the story, while showing the development that has taken place to make this memory meaningful.

Realisation
Realisation in a character can reflect new awareness in the reader, creating a strong effect. A closing line, where the narrator supposes or suspects something new, is often more forceful than a direct statement. For example, 'I suppose when people lie they always blink more than once' is more telling than, 'I know he was a liar.'

There are as many approaches as there are short stories. Analyse your favourite stories and see how they work to a good closing line. In the best stories there will be entirely new ways of ending, created specifically for this story.

Finally, to avoid the wrath of editors, never, ever close your story with The End.

REWRITING CREATIVELY

Rewriting is part of the creative process, and can transform poor and average stories into something exceptional.

When rewriting you should routinely check:

- spelling
- grammar
- the logic of your plot and ideas
- realism
- originality of images.

Having spent so much time and effort writing your story, it is tempting to view a first draft as somehow untouchable. In reality all stories benefit from editing, so you should revise thoroughly and rewrite ruthlessly. Your story as a whole is more important than any single line, image or phrase. Be willing to cut out favourite sentences and words if they don't genuinely contribute to your story.

Some people find that leaving the story for a few days helps to give them perspective. When you come back to your story after a break the errors, flaws and discrepancies stand out more than they could during the first bursts of creativity.

Fine tuning a story

Rewriting consists of fine tuning your work by:

- cutting
- reordering
- adding new words.

Ask yourself if every sentence is the best it could be. Are there any changes you could make, to give it more relevance to the story, a more consistent style, a better sound? See Figure 3 for an example.

FINDING A TITLE

Once a piece has been written and edited it is tempting to rush it into the post. This sort of haste can lead to work being sent out with bland, irrelevant titles. If your title is intriguing, original and expressive, it will help to sell your story, so it's worth putting in some more thought.

1. A title should communicate information, but it should also sound good, intriguing readers. Popular phrases and quotations are an excellent source of title ideas, as with *Ringing the Changes, Get a Life, Level Crossing*.

The following example reads quite well, but see if you can determine where the changes could take place.

'Rachel's eyes didn't appear to be focused on him any more. One of them looked like it was crying. Stuart smiled, because he thought she was smiling at him, but it took only a moment to realise she was wincing with pain. Letting go of her hand, her skin stuck to his. Her palm was covered with blisters, which gave off something the colour of honey. He wiped the stuff onto the sheet, then walked off hurriedly towards the door.'

By making a few simple cuts, deleting adverbs, reordering and making better word choices, this can be made more readable.

'Rachel's eyes were unfocused, shining with tears. When her mouth turned up, he smiled back, then realised she was wincing with pain. Letting go of her hand, her skin stuck to his. Her palm was blotted with blisters, which leaked something the colour of honey. He wiped the mucus onto the sheet, then backed off towards the door.'

Take your time, and read out loud if necessary, to see where the pauses, jolts and unnatural sounds lie in your sentences. Cut out unnecessary words and make every sentence earn its place.

Fig. 3.   How to fine tune your story.

2. Puns, such as *Fission Impossible, The Futility Room* and *The Comfort of Stranglers*, are common, but be wary of sounding too tabloid.

3. Alliteration can be effective. *The Black Burns* and *Domino Dreams* are both simple titles, but the repeated letters make them sound impressive.

4. Titles should always be relevant to your story. If you think up a wonderful phrase, such as *The Colour Purple* or *Look Back*

in Anger, only use it if it is truly relevant. Although you are free to experiment with expression, ensure that it enhances, rather than confuses, your fiction.

Using key words

Sometimes key words or phrases from within stories work, as with *The Mathematics of the Night* and *Because of Dust*.

Snippets of dialogue taken out of context are also interesting, but make sure they are important pieces of conversation which sum up the story. *Don't Wake Up, Leave Me Alone* and *What Happens Now?* are all sections of dialogue that became titles.

Powerful juxtapositions are common. *Shaved Fish, Sugar Sleep* and *The Fatal Bodice* all work, because the contrast is unusual and makes the reader want to know more.

Readers hold titles in their minds, as a key to a story or poem, so make sure your title reflects a story's meaning. The title should be memorable, as well as enhancing the story's main theme.

CHECKLIST

● Choose an ending that does more than summarise your story.

● Use anti-climax to settle the story, following action.

● Show how your character has developed.

● Resolve the plot through action, rather than decision.

● Find a suitable title.

● Keep a thesaurus and book of quotations to hand.

● Set your story aside for a while, before rewriting.

● Cut ruthlessly, honing each sentence.

CASE STUDIES

Peter closes the story

While writing Peter realises that the story is reaching a natural conclusion. He drives it towards the final action, where Brian is forced to take a risk, removing the Blocker himself. Although this is the final action, Peter realises that for the reader to see the change in Brian another short scene is required. He writes a few closing paragraphs, showing Brian days later, in a different situation. Rather than showing him playing the piano again, which would be too corny, a reference is made to a forthcoming performance. At first this scene is too long so he cuts it during the rewrite, giving the story a sense of balance.

Michael rewrites thoroughly
Michael's story doesn't have an obvious ending, so he keeps writing, letting the plot develop. Eventually, when he finds a suitable resolution, he realises that many of the middle-section scenes can be cut, giving the story a more snappy pace. He rewrites the whole story, cutting out scenes that don't contribute and tightening his writing throughout. He experiments with several closing lines, eventually opting for dialogue. The short speech, which comes soon after the main action, adds new meaning to the story but also makes it feel complete.

Ruth finds a title
With the story complete Ruth goes over the whole manuscript, striking out unnecessary words and reordering sentences. She then sets the story aside for a few days. When she comes to read through it again she spots several more mistakes and also finds that the ending is too abrupt. It makes sense, but it happens so quickly that the reader is left feeling empty. She fills out the closing page with an extra scene of interaction, making sure that she doesn't simply pad the story out. She then takes several lines at random from the page, combining words until she finds a suitable title.

DISCUSSION POINTS

1. What is the last thing that happens in your story, in terms of plot? How soon after this will the story end?

2. Write several closing lines. Do some of these close the story, more than end it? Do any of them add something new to the story?

3. Rewrite your story, fine tuning sentences. How will this help you when you next write a story?

4. Write down a selection of titles for your story. Which would intrigue readers the most? Does your title reflect the story's content?

5. Look back at your original notes. How far have you come since the original idea? Has the story achieved everything you wanted it to?

11
Selling Science Fiction

Whether you write stories or novels, you want your work to be read. Science fiction, fantasy and horror are popular, with avid readers and enthusiastic editors. Selling short stories is easier than novels and it will help if you gain a reputation in the field. If you approach an editor with your first novel, showing a list of previous story sales, it can certainly help with the way you are received.

IDENTIFYING YOUR MARKET

The secret to selling your work is finding the right market for each story. Every publication has its own house style, which must be adhered to. The key is market study.

> Whether you enter a competition, submit to a magazine, or approach a book editor, you should know what type of work they are looking for.

You will hardly ever sell science fiction to magazines with a general readership, so it is a waste of time sending it to them. Once you have found a science fiction magazine, you must be aware of their preferences. Some magazines like hard SF, with lots of metal and technology, while others prefer a more fantastical approach. Some may be open to horror, while others will shun it. While some magazines will love the mention of virtual reality, others will dismiss it as old-fashioned.

At the very least buy one copy of the magazine you intend to write for and read the stories it contains. Ideally, ask for the magazine's guidelines. These are sometimes vague, but always help to an extent. Having studied these you can write a story to suit the magazine's style, or look through your file of stories to find something suitable.

Before sending off check that your story is suitable in terms of:

- subject matter
- characterisation
- theme
- length
- title
- style of writing
- overall tone.

In each case, check that you have covered these areas in a way that will appeal to a particular magazine.

There are four main outlets for short stories.

Small press magazines

By far the easiest way to get published is through small press magazines. They range from photocopied pages through to glossy, modern designs, covering a huge range of tastes and quality. Although these magazines are read by only a few hundred people these sometimes include professional editors, publishers and literary critics, along with SF enthusiasts.

Although breaking into the small press is comparatively easy, editors won't take a story from you simply because you send it in. If you identify your market correctly, write appropriately and to the best of your ability, you stand a good chance of being accepted.

Payment is almost negligible, often in contributors' copies of the magazine, rather than cash. The real reward is seeing your work in print, reading subsequent reviews and readers' letters, and developing a reputation. Editorial decisions can take a couple of months, but sometimes they come within days. The editors are helpful, and will either point you in a suitable direction or advise you on how to improve your stories. They try to avoid standard rejection letters and, when time permits, reply in detail.

Semi-professional magazines

Semi-professional magazines, such as *Interzone*, are much more difficult to break into, although rejection letters may contain useful advice. The competition is incredibly fierce, and it is absolutely vital that you study the market and tune your work accordingly.

Anthologies

Anthologies are an excellent and underestimated way to break into publishing, because book editors love to slip in new talent amongst the big names. Many, such as *Year's Best Fantasy and Horror* (DAW Books), and *Best New Horror*, only republish work, but some are open to unpublished stories. These tend to be irregular and it will take some detective work to track them down. By joining some of the societies mentioned at the back, and establishing contact with other writers and editors, you will stand more chance of finding out about such anthologies. You can even try writing to publishing companies with a speculative query.

Writing competitions

Writing competitions are often open to science fiction, fantasy and horror, so long as you avoid clichés or extreme styles. The key to winning writing competitions is a balance of originality and polish. Competition judges are usually looking for promise in a writer, so if you can craft a story, while writing originally, SF, fantasy and horror can win. Read the rules carefully though, and read past winners' stories to determine what type of story usually wins, to avoid wasting your own time and money.

PRESENTING WORK

Wherever you send your work, present it professionally. Handwritten, badly typed or scruffy pages will be rejected immediately by most editors. Take the time to present yourself professionally. Editors care about content more than presentation, but they will be more willing to read a manuscript if it has been put together with care.

Using a computer

If you plan to spend a lot of time writing, you will find that a computer is essential. With minimal effort you will be able to present typeset, quality manuscripts in minutes.

Writing on a word-processor is easier than typing, because you are free to chop and shift text, adding words and reordering as you write. It's a more creative and homogenous process than typing or handwriting. Your stories are also stored, and filed on disc, which makes keeping track of your submissions easy. Writers also make great use of spelling and grammar checkers, along with the automatic word count facilities.

A professional approach is essential, even if you are writing as a minor hobby. When editors see a neat, word-processed document, they know you are serious. Many also like to take submissions on disc (alongside a printed copy), to enable their typesetter to do a clean and speedy job.

Although you can use any type of IBM-compatible PC, most writers favour Apple Macintosh computers, as they are most prevalent in the publishing industry. As for software, you can't go wrong with Word 6.0, or something similar.

Printing out your story

When a story has been fully edited, and is ready for sending off, print it out and make sure that you:

- use A4 white paper
- double space the lines
- leave an unjustified right-hand edge
- spell and grammar check thoroughly
- leave wide margins all round
- include page number, name and title on each page
- use a new printer cartridge
- bind with a paper clip; never use staples.

Each story should contain a covering sheet which states:

- the title of the story
- your name and address
- the approximate word count of the story.

Handling copyright

Your cover sheet can also include a brief copyright notice, such as © 1997 Christopher Kenworthy. This is not a legal requirement, because copyright is automatically yours the moment you write something down, but this will show editors that you are a serious writer.

The covering sheet should also state which rights are being offered. This means that when you sell a story you give somebody permission to publish your story, under certain conditions. When writing short stories, you will probably only sell:

The Running Sore

Jacob Klines

5600 words

Disposable manuscript

First English Language Rights

1 Jones Drive
Smithstone
Amberside
Wiltshire
W23 5XZ

Tel/Fax 01234 123456
jacob@klass.sample.com.uk

Fig. 4.   Sample cover sheet.

- First British Serial Rights (an unpublished story in a British magazine)

- First North American Rights (an unpublished story in a US magazine)

- First English Language Rights (first publication of a story in the world)

- Reprint Rights (republishing a story elsewhere).

Copyright needn't be complicated, and editors will rarely try to cheat you, so be willing to take their advice. To keep it really simple, just type First English Language Rights on the covering sheet. If the editors want something else, they will let you know.

Unless an editor offers you a lot of money, avoid selling All Rights. If your story is a success the owner of the rights can sell it again and again, forever, without your permission and without paying you another penny.

APPROACHING EDITORS

Editors are human, but they are amongst the busiest people on earth. Although they may be interested in your past writing success they are not bothered about your exams results, social background, country of origin, or literary aims. Don't bore them with a long letter. Your letter should include your name, address and the title of the story. Mention previous publishing history, here relevant, and if you have a recent issue of the magazine you can mention that, but don't crawl. Your letter needn't be any more complicated than the one in Figure 5.

You will be tempted to describe your story, explaining what it means to you, who it will appeal to and so on. Don't. Stick to the facts. Editors want to get on with story reading, so give them a chance.

Don't try to be over friendly with editors, using their first name, unless you have corresponded for a while. Don't try to be funny. Even small press publishers take their magazines seriously and will be more impressed by an understated approach.

Jacob Klines

1 Jones Drive   Smithstone   Amberside
Wiltshire   W23 5XZ
Tel/Fax 01234 123456
jacob@klass.sample.com.uk

Andy Cox, Editor
The Third Alternative
5 Martins Lane
Witcham
Ely
Cambs
CB6 2LB

May 8, 199X

Dear Mr Cox

I enjoyed the recent issue of *The Third Alternative*, and would like to submit a story for publication. Please find enclosed *The Running Sore*, which is 5600 words long. An SAE is enclosed for your reply.

Yours sincerely

Jacob Klines

Jacob Klines

Fig. 5. Sample covering letter to an editor.

Including an SAE

Always include a stamped, self-addressed envelope (SAE) with any submission or letter of enquiry. If you don't, your work will be thrown away and your reputation will be damaged. Use quality envelopes and sufficient postage.

Presentation is important, right down to the SAE, but remember that you are a writer not a designer.

● Make your manuscript production system as efficient as possible, or you will waste valuable writing time.

Understanding payment

Payment for science fiction, fantasy and horror stories ranges from a free copy of the magazine through to hundreds of pounds. Sometimes a new novel will sell for just 2,000, and in other cases the writer will be offered hundreds of thousands. When you begin writing, expect little or no payment.

Although science fiction can provide you with a substantial income, it is your writing that matters. Concentrate on writing more fiction, improving all the time, and the payment should improve of its own accord.

Selling novels

The process for selling novels is almost identical, except that it can take longer. When you send off a novel it will probably be read by a professional reader. If the reader gives it a glowing report the editor will read it, and a decision will be made. Unless your manuscript is stunningly good or bad you will wait at least two months, and often twice as long.

Finding an agent

Agents don't sell short stories, unless you are extremely famous. They will take on new novel writers. A good agent will:

● get your manuscript read more quickly
● sort out legal matters
● obtain a good deal, with a fair contract
● pay for the postage and printing of your manuscript
● help to guide your career.

On the negative side, an agent will take approximately 10 per cent of your earnings from the book. You should remember that agents can't sell bad books. If you have written a good novel it will probably sell, whether or not you have an agent.

Finding an agent is similar to finding a publisher, and almost as difficult. You will find a list of agents in *The Writer's Handbook*. Send them a brief letter of enquiry and, if they are open to your suggestion, send the complete manuscript. A decision should come within a couple of months.

PROMOTING YOURSELF

Even if you are writing exclusively for small press magazines, you will gain a reputation. People will begin to notice your name, and if they enjoy your work they will look forward to reading more. This makes you attractive to editors, who want to sell their magazines. This in turn helps you to sell stories elsewhere. With a few small press sales you can break into professional magazines. This then helps you to sell a novel.

To ptomote yourself effectively, write a short paragraph of biographical details. This should include your

- name
- age
- interests
- employment
- past experience
- and relevant story sales.

Write this as an informal statement about the writer you are, rather than as a CV.

As your sales build the biography will make editors more relaxed about reading your work. It also saves them asking for you to send it in separately, as most magazines publish such details alongside the story.

Most fiction magazines contain letters pages. It is worth contributing to these, as they keep your name in the public eye and show that you are serious about fiction.

Coping with rejection

All writers receive rejection letters. Usually these are printed forms, saying that the editors didn't like your story but unfortunately don't have time to explain why. In some cases boxes will be ticked, showing which areas of your story could be improved. The most thoughtful editors will write brief letters of advice.

When rejection letters come accept them as part of the writing life. Sometimes the advice can be extremely helpful, even if it seems hurtful at first. If a story is rejected, consider rewriting it and then send it somewhere else.

WRITING SOMETHING NEW

This book has effectively detailed the writing of one short story. To be a successful writer you will want to write hundreds of stories, or several novels. With practise writing will become easier and quicker.

> To be a successful writer you should *live* as a writer, constantly observing. You should find time to write, and you should keep writing, no matter how discouraging the rejections, delays and mistakes.

Once a story is complete, write another. Don't wait for a rejection or acceptance before writing something new. Get straight into the next story.

The techniques, suggestions and examples in this book should help you to write powerful science fiction, fantasy and horror stories. In time you will learn your own style. You will learn to edit and rewrite, while you create. Eventually many of the techniques will become second nature.

Practise writing every day, and keep trying. With persistence you can write stories that sell.

CHECKLIST

- Identify the most suitable market for each story you write.

- Present your work as professionally as possible.

- Write brief, precise letters to editors.

- Promote yourself within the small press.

- Always enclose an SAE with your submission.

- Consider the advice in rejection letters.

- Practise writing every day.

CASE STUDIES

Peter sends off his story

Peter feels that he could go on revising his story forever, but realises that he is stalling. He completes the story to the best of his ability, then prints it out, sends it off and waits. In the meantime he begins writing letters to agents and publishers, so that his name will be known when he comes to write a novel. He is already making notes about his ideas.

Michael promotes himself

While rounding his story off Michael makes himself known to editors, by writing to letter pages. He writes about the type of fiction he is interested in, sparking off a debate in the small press. This makes people eager to read his work, to see exactly what he means. When his first story is complete he prints it out, puts together the package of letter, biography and SAE, then sends it off.

Ruth writes something new

Having printed her story Ruth sends it off and immediately begins work on something new. She is keen to know what the editor thinks, but accepts that if rejected she will be able to learn from the experience. While making notes she realises how much she has learnt about the writing process. Her sentences, images and dialogue are already more realistic and flowing.

DISCUSSION POINTS

1. Find a potential market for your story. Do you need to change the title, length or style, to make it more suitable? Is there a better market?

2. Print out your story and letter. Is your manuscript clean and clear?

3. Write something new. How has your writing technique developed since you first began? How can you improve from here?

Glossary

Alien. A non-human creature from another planet.

Alliteration. The repetition of consonant sounds at the beginning of words, as in 'beneath the burnished bridge'. This is especially useful for titles.

Alternate world. A fictional version of the world, based on a slightly altered history.

Android. An artificial humanoid, designed to be like a human.

Artificial intelligence (AI). A machine which is capable of intelligent thought. Although computer simulations of intelligence are already possible to an extent, science fiction explores the idea that computers may one day be conscious. If this was the case computers might have personality, soul and could even be granted civil rights.

Artificial lifeforms. Living entities which have been designed and constructed, but which are capable of reproduction.

Blurb. A descriptive passage on a book jacket, advertising the contents. Blurb also refers to the words of praise for a book, quoted from reviewers and authors on a book jacket.

Characterisation. Giving the people of a story distinctive and consistent personalities.

Cliché. An expression that has lost its force through over-use, such as 'towering trees', or 'rippling muscles'. Although cliché can add realism to dialogue when used sparingly, it should be avoided at other times. Cliché also refers to ideas that are unoriginal.

Cyborg. A mechanically adapted human, whose limbs, organs and even brain have been replaced with artificial devices, which may enhance abilities.

Cyberpunk. A sub-genre of hard SF, popular in the 1980s, led by writers such as William Gibson and Bruce Serling. It concentrates on under-the-skin technology, with computer-dominated futures run by corporations. Heavy on 'street' style, with characters who were more surface than substance, cyberpunk remains influential on television and movie SF, although its role in literature has diminished.

Deus ex machina. An unexpected, artificial, or improbable event introduced suddenly in a story to resolve a situation or untangle a plot. *Deus ex machina* spoils stories, because it reduces the importance of a character's actions.

Dystopia. An imaginary future in which life is extremely bad because of deprivation, oppression or terror.

Fantasy. A genre of fiction characterised by highly fanciful or supernatural elements. The most basic form of fantasy deals with sword and sorcery, world of magic, with battles of good against evil. Fantasy can also be set in more ordinary surroundings, where reality is slightly blurred and altered through different states of mind or the application of magic.

Faster than light travel. Any form of transport that exceeds the speed of light, by exotic methods such as warping space.

First contact. The moment when humans and aliens first come into contact. A mainstay of SF, this idea can be tackled in many ways, from alien visitation through to Earth travellers invading another planet. The protocols and ethics of first contact stories still have potential for SF writers.

Free energy. The idea that a scientific discovery will effectively make a renewable, clean, inexpensive form of energy available. Cold fusion, for instance, would create enough energy to power the world, from a cupful of seawater. Whether this energy is actually free, or controlled by individuals and corporations, determines the way this idea is used in SF.

Gene. A hereditary unit contained within the DNA of cells, which determines physical characteristics. Gene mutation, replication and alteration is the basis for many SF stories.

Genetic engineering. The deliberate mutation or splicing of genes, to alter the nature of offspring.

Genre. A category of literature marked by a distinctive style, form or content. People working in the fields of speculative fiction often refer exclusively to science fiction, fantasy and horror as 'genre'.

Gore. Extreme form of horror, in which the emphasis is on vivid descriptions of physical suffering, such as disembowelment and mutilation.

Hard SF. A brand of science fiction characterised by emphasis on plausible technology. Although speculative it elaborates known science, detailing ideas such as spaceships, hardwiring the brain, and the terraforming of planets.

Heightened realism. A modern form of slipstream writing, in which SF, fantasy and horror are woven into the ordinary, contemporary world. This creates a sense of realism which is so extreme that it can be dreamlike.

Horror. Fiction that frightens the reader, often with supernatural elements.

Imagery. The use of expressive or evocative images in fiction. More specifically, imagery refers to the sensory descriptions that help a reader to visualise the story.

Juxtaposition. Placing two things close together, to show their contrast.

Magic realism. A form of fiction which contains symbolic and bizarre images and ideas, alongside ordinary events. Magic realism is often plotless, with the logic of a story being dictated by a character's thoughts and beliefs as much as by action. Similiar to heightened realism, but often more portentous and less intense.

Miserablism. An area of fiction where mainstream literature is combined with SF, fantasy and horror. Although its mood is often dark and urban, it is also humorous.

Motif. A recurrent image, phrase or thematic element in fiction.

Mutation. The changing of a creature's genetic make-up to form a new type of being, usually as offspring.

Nano-technology. This branch of science concerns extremely small machines, sometimes made of a few atoms, which work at the molecular level. In theory it should be possible to inject self-replicating nano machines into a body, to repair damaged cells, strengthen weak cells and renew bone. Nano machines could also be used to manufacture complex materials and foods from waste products.

Pace. The rate of speed at which a story proceeds. A good story will usually move between steady and quick pacing.

Parallel world. A separate reality, which exists alongside ours. In SF a parallel world can be a slightly different version of our reality, or entirely different planets which can be reached through certain crossover points. Specific conditions need to be met, in most cases, for the crossover to take place.

Plot. The sequence of events in a story which forms the main story line.

Science fiction. A literary genre based on speculative scientific discoveries or developments. It is concerned with environmental changes, space travel, life on other planets and other speculations, all of which ask what the world would be like if things were different.

Slipstream. A form of cross-genre SF, concerned more with mood, atmosphere and characterisation than hard plot and science. Often published in mainstream magazines, slipstream is enjoyed by SF readers because of the weird and unusual elements which colour it.

Small press. Many small magazines, run independently by enthusiasts, are collectively termed the small press.

Soft SF. Science fiction which deals with states of mind, politics and personality, rather than hard science or technology.

Space opera. A form of SF, which shows a hero battling against the odds through extreme drama. Movies such as *Star Wars* are classic examples of how space opera can entertain, while Colin Greenland's novel *Take Back Plenty* shows how this form still has much to offer.

Splatterpunk. A style of horror, which emphasises vivid descriptions of physical violence.

Steampunk. A sub-genre of science fiction, in which an alternate view of history is shown. What if, for example, Hitler had won the Second World War, or if nuclear power had been discovered two hundred years ago?

Sword and sorcery. A type of fiction in which mythical and magical beings battle between good and evil.

Sub-plot. A story that runs alongside, but in harmony with, the main plot.

Teleportation. A theoretical form of transport, in which the body is broken down into energy, beamed to another place and reorganised to its original form.

Terraforming. The process of making other planets, such as Mars, habitable for human colonisation by changing the atmosphere and surface, and introducing life.

Theme. The overall meaning of a story.

Utopia. An imaginary future in which life is extremely pleasant, and all of our contemporary problems (such as war and famine) have been solved. Ironically, Utopian societies are often portrayed as being extremely unpleasant in SF.

Virtual reality. Advanced simulations, in which all the senses are catered for, so that the events simulated (such as flying) seem absolutely real. In SF virtual reality is used to control remote robots, as entertainment, and to provide alternate realities.

Warp drive. An engine system built into a spaceship, which allows it to warp space and thus travel faster than the speed of light.

Useful Addresses

SOCIETIES AND ASSOCIATIONS

The British Fantasy Society. Membership of the BFS is £17 per annum. You receive a bi-monthly newsletter, a regular magazine of new stories and the benefit of being in contact with hundreds of like-minded writers and fans. The annual British Fantasy Convention is always memorable, not only for the awards ceremony and banquet, but for the invaluable contacts. The professionals mingle with newcomers and the atmosphere is unique. Obtain details by sending an SAE to the BFS Secretary, 2 Harwood Street, Stockport SK4 1JJ.

The British Science Fiction Association. The BSFA covers SF and related genres, and is aimed at authors, publishers and fans. Membership is £18 per annum, for which you receive three magazines which cover news and information, amateur fiction and critical studies. Most importantly, the BSFA organises an Orbiter group, which allows members to study each others' fiction, offering support and constructive criticism. Details from Alison Cook, 52 Wood Hill Drive, Grove, Wantage, Oxfordshire OX12 0DF.

The Gothic Society. A quarterly newsletter and magazine are produced by The Gothic Society, along with relevant book lists and information. Membership is £20 per year. The Gothic Society, Chatham House, Gosshill Road, Chiselhurst, Kent BR7 5NS. Tel: (0181) 467 8475.

The Ghost Story Society. Devoted to supernatural fiction, especially traditional ghost stories, this society supplies members with three magazines each year, detailing new books, movies and television shows. It also publishers letters and new fiction. Membership is £13.50 per year. The Ghost Story Society, Ashcroft, 2 Abbottsford Drive, Penyffordd, Chester CH4 0JG.

115

Ansible. David Langford's humorous SF newsletter is available free. Send an SAE to 94 London Road, Reading, Berkshire RG1 5AU.

SERVICES

Freelance Press Services. Offers a variety of services for writers, and supplies how-to write books via mail order. Freelance Press Services, Cumberland House, Lissadel Street, Salford M6 6GG. Tel: (0161) 702 8225.

The Association of Freelance Writers. Offers services and support for writers. The Association of Freelance Writers, Sevendale House, 7 Dale Street, Manchester M1 1JB. Tel: (0161) 228 2362.

COURSES

Arvon Foundation. The Arvon Foundation runs five-day residential writing courses at centres in Yorkshire, Devon and Inverness-shire. Students work with professional writers, in groups and individually. There are many general fiction writing courses, and occasionally Arvon runs courses that specialise in science fiction, fantasy and horror. For a brochure send an SAE to The Arvon Foundation at Lumb Bank, Hebden Bridge, West Yorkshire HX7 6DF.

Indian King Arts Centre. Residential writing courses are run throughout the year, sometimes specialising in SF, fantasy and horror. For a brochure contact The Indian King Arts Centre, Fore Street, Calemford, Cornwall PL32 9PG.

Further Reading

FICTION MAGAZINES

The Third Alternative, edited by Andy Cox, is probably the best slipstream magazine, specialising in borderline horror, SF and magic/heightened realism. Single issue £2.50, four-issue subscription £9. Cheques payable to The Third Alternative, 5 Martins Lane, Witcham, Ely, Cambridgeshire CB6 2LB.

Peeping Tom, edited by Stuart Hughes, published by David Bell, contains a mixed bag of extreme horror, from new and big-name writers, with occasional gems. Four-issue subscription £7.50. Cheques payable to Peeping Tom, Yew Tree House, 15 Nottingham Rd, Ashby de la Zouch, Leicestershire LE65 1DJ.

Interzone, edited by David Pringle, is Britain's premier science fiction publication, containing new stories, reviews and critical articles. Single issue £2.50, twelve-issue subscription £28. Cheques payable to Interzone, 217 Preston Drove, Brighton BN1 6FL.

BBR, edited by Chris Reed, is experimental in tone, but still concentrates on plot-driven, moody SF. The editor can also provide details of The New Science Fiction Alliance, which supplies copies of foreign and difficult to obtain magazines. Single copy £3.50, four-issue subscription £11. Cheques payable to Chris Reed, BBR, PO Box 625, Sheffield S1 3GY.

Dreams From The Stranger's Café, edited by John Gaunt, is a well produced magazine of obscure and surreal fiction, often with elements of science fiction. Single issue £2.50, four-issue subscription £9. Cheques to John Gaunt, 15 Clifton Grove, Clifton, Rotherham, South Yorkshire S65 2AZ.

Substance, edited by Paul Beardsley, publishes all types of science fiction with the emphasis on technological, plot-driven stories.

Single issue £2.50, four-issue subscription £9. Cheques to Neville Barnes, 65 Conbar Avenue, Rustington, West Sussex BN16 3LZ.

Kimota is the magazine for the Preston SF Group, editor Graeme Hurry. Manages to publish a broad range of SF, fantasy and horror, along with articles and artwork. Although famous writers appear here, the editor is open to new writers. Single issue £2, four-issue subscription £7. Cheques to Kimota Publishing, 52 Cadley Causeway, Preston, Lancashire PR2 3RX.

MAGAZINES FOR WRITERS

Zene comes from the same publishers as *The Third Alternative*, and contains guidelines for other magazines to which writers can submit stories. It also publishes reviews and non-fiction articles. Single issue £1.95, four-issue subscription £7. Cheques to *Zene*, 5 Martins Lane, Witcham, Ely, Cambridgeshire CB6 2LB.

Freelance Market News publishes lists of new markets and competitions for writers. Six-issue subscription £13.95, eleven-issue subscription £25. Cheques to Freelance Press Services, Cumberland House, Lissadel Street, Salford M6 6GG.

Writers' Forum, edited by John Benton, publishes a range of how-to-write articles. Single issue £3.35 from Writers' Forum, 9/10 Roberts Close, Moxley, Wednesbury, West Midlands WS10 8SS.

Writer's News and *Writing Magazine*, edited by Richard Bell, cover all aspects of writing, in terms of craft and publication. A twelve-month subscription to both is £41.60. Cheques to Writer's News Ltd, PO Box 4, Nairn, Inverness-shire IV12 4HU.

Writer's Monthly covers all aspects of writing, with the majority of articles detailing fiction technique. For subscription details contact (0181) 347 6778.

Write Lines is the magazine for *The Association of Freelance Writers*, giving market news alongside how-to-write articles. Details of membership and subscription rates from The Association of Freelance Writers, Sevendale House, 7 Dale Street, Manchester M1 1JB. Tel: (0161) 228 2362.

RECOMMENDED FICTION

Arc d'X, Steve Erickson.
Blind Needle, Trevor Hoyle.
The Child Garden, Geoff Ryman.
The Count of Eleven, Ramsey Campbell.
The Course of The Heart, M. John Harrison.
The Earth Wire, Joel Lane.
The Earthsea Trilogy, Ursula Le Guin.
Exquisite Corpse, Robert Irwin.
Finishing Touches, Thomas Tessier.
Head Injuries, Conrad Williams.
House of Lost Dreams, Graham Joyce.
The Ice Monkey, M. John Harrison.
The Immaculate, Mark Morris.
Koko, Peter Straub.
Little Deaths, ed. Ellen Datlow.
Lord of The Rings, J. R. R. Tolkien.
Mr Badface, Mark Morris.
Only Forward, Michael Marshall Smith.
Outside the Dog Museum, Jonathan Carroll.
The Prestige, Christopher Priest.
Red Mars, Kim Stanley Robinson.
Saxophone Dreams, Nicholas Royle.
The Search, Geoff Dyer.
Spider, patrick McGrath.
Take Back Plenty, Colin Greenland.
Vurt, Jeff Noon.
Was, Geoff Ryman.
Will You Hold Me?, Chris Kenworthy.
The Year's Best Fantasy and Horror, ed. Ellen Datlow.

ESSENTIAL REFERENCE

The Encyclopaedia of Science Fiction, John Clute, (St Martin's
    Griffin).
The Writers' Handbook, (Macmillan).
The Writers' and Artists' Yearbook, (A & C Black).

A selection of other How To Books for writers
Creative Writing: How to develop your writing skills for successful

fiction and nonfiction work, Adèle Ramet (How To Books, 1996).

Copyright & Law for Writers: How to protect yourself and your creative work, Helen Shay (How To Books, 1996).

How to Write for Television, William Smethurst (How To Books, 1992).

Writing & Selling a Novel: How to craft your fiction for publication, Marina Oliver (How To Books, 1996).

How to Write for Publication, Chriss McCallum (How To Books, 3rd edition 1995). A comprehensive reference manual.

Index

COPYRIGHT & LAW FOR WRITERS
How to protect yourself and your creative work

Helen Shay

This book will be a useful tool for any writer, but especially invaluable to beginners and those just starting to enjoy some success. Make sure you never receive any legal short change. This book takes you through the main legal implications relevant to writers, from first putting pen to paper/finger to keyboard through to selling work, entering a contract and onto collecting the full financial rewards due to you. It also explains exactly what to do if things go wrong. It explains the various pitfalls and how to steer clear of them – for example copyright infringement – whilst showing how to preserve your own rights, and learning how to publish and not be damned. A graduate of Manchester University, Helen Shay is a qualified solicitor of twelve years' standing. Currently working in an ombudsman's office in London, she is well-versed in the problems which can confront the individual versus large organisations. She also tutors and lectures part-time in business law. She is a member of the Society of Women Writers and Journalists and the Women Writers Network, and currently writes a regular legal column for *Writers News*.

96pp. illus. 1 85703 416 3.

WRITING REVIEWS
How to write about arts and leisure for pleasure and profit

Carole Baldock

Imagine enjoying all your favourite leisure activities for free – eating out and visiting tourist attractions, going to exhibitions and concerts, theatre and cinema, or being entertained in the comfort of your own home with new books, CDs and the latest video releases. Newspapers and magazines of all kinds have a huge appetite for reviews, much of which is written by freelancers. This book shows you how to break into the reviewing market, how to set up, how to conduct research and interviews, how to draft your review and tailor it to the appropriate media, and how to use reviewing for personal networking and skills-building. Carole Baldock BA(Hons) is herself a highly experienced freelance reviewer whose work has appeared throughout the national and provincial press and in specialist publications of many kinds.

160pp. illus. 1 85703 441 4.

HOW TO START WORD PROCESSING
A step-by-step guide for beginners

Ian Phillipson

In the modern world an ability to wordprocess is a valuable, even essential, skill. It opens up new career opportunities, allows you to do your job so much better, and to complete all kinds of assignments far more quickly and effectively. Even if you know little or nothing about modern technology, this book will help you, because it deals with basic principles. If you want to design and print out simple letters and documents, produce mailshots, or explore desk top publishing, then this is the book for you, complete with case studies and checklists to help you on your way. Ian Phillipson is an experienced DTP and business consultant, with a range of business and professional clients in both the public and private sectors.

124pp. illus. 1 85703 156 3.

CREATING A TWIST IN THE TALE
How to write successful short stories for women's magazines

Adèle Ramet

For the short story writer, the twist in the tale offers excellent opportunities for publication. It is fun to write and, at 500–1200 words in length, relatively economical to produce. Best of all, the market for twist stories grows with each new women's title that appears on the newsagent's shelves. However, achieving the twist in a story's tail isn't nearly so easy as it looks. Misleading by their very nature, these stories can foil attempts of even the most experienced unless they know the tricks of the trade. This book dispels the myths and misconceptions surrounding the art of writing twist stories. It will guide you step-by-step to use characterisation, viewpoint, flashback and dialogue to maximum effect. You will learn the art of 'twist signposting' and how to write backwards but most importantly of all, this book will give you all the information you need to develop that vital ingredient for success – a creatively twisted mind. Adèle Ramet is Chairman of the South Eastern Writers Association and an experienced creative writing tutor. She has contributed widely to *Bella, Woman's Realm*, and many other leading woman's magazines.

124pp. illus. 1 85703 411 2.

HOW TO WRITE FOR PUBLICATION
Your practical guide to success

Chriss McCallum

'How can I sell my work? How do I protect my copyright? Can a magazine steal my story? Why just a printed rejection slip – can't editors tell me where I'm going wrong? Are writing courses worth the money? Should I get an agent?' Highly expert and practical, **How to write for Publication** gives the often surprising answers to these and hundreds of other questions most often asked by the great silent majority of struggling writers, whether of fiction, nonfiction, poetry, drama, stories or articles. No author seriously interested in getting published can afford to be without this manual, packed with checklists, examples and key contacts. 'Handy for both professional and newcomer alike.' *Writers News*. 'Everything you ever wanted to know about the practical side of publishing . . . excellent.' *Competitors Journal*. 'Really definitive . . . Leaves every other similar book in its shade.' *Pause (National Poetry Foundation)*. 'It is, quite simply, one of the best books of its kind that I've ever read.' Steve Wetton, Author of BBC TV's comedy drama *Growing Pains*. 'The revised edition maintains the high standard . . . Its reference section of useful addresses is value for money on its own.' *Writers News*. Chriss McCallum has many years' experience as a professional Editor, and has worked for Collins, Penguin, W H Allen and other leading firms. She was publisher of *The Writers Voice* (1983–86) and is a Member of the Society of Authors, The Society of Women Writers & Journalists, and an Honorary Member of the Comedy Writers Association.

192pp. illus. 1 85703 140 7. 3rd edition.

STARTING TO WRITE
How to create written work for publication and profit

Marina & Deborah Oliver

How does a writer get started? How do writers manage the physical aspects? This new book shows would-be writers how to look at their motives, how to set realistic objectives, and how to devise a plan of action without wasting time and resources. Illustrated throughout with case studies, it will show you how to explore various options, discover what methods work best for you, and take advantage of tips from experienced writers. Start now, and learn how to get your work into print. Marina Oliver has written and published over 30 novels, published her own magazine, written and edited many booklets, and taught creative writing. Deborah Oliver has edited a monthly magazine and is currently production editor of a computer magazine.

124pp. illus. 1 85703 401 5.

WRITING & SELLING A NOVEL
How to craft your fiction for publication

Marina Oliver

Writing a novel seems a daunting task until attempted. Marina Oliver's invaluable, eminently practical book, based on firsthand experience, offers realistic encouragement, down to earth advice, expert tips and suggestions to guide aspiring novelists. They include how to get started, the key elements to consider, where to look for help, how to approach publishers and what to expect during the process of publication. A former further education lecturer, and tutor for creative writing courses, Marina Oliver has published over 30 novels, short, long, historical and contemporary. Chairman of the Romantic Novelists' Association 1991–3, and an adviser to the 1994 edition of the biographical dictionary, *Twentieth Century Romance and Historical Writers*, she lectures widely on writing.

144pp. illus. 1 85703 406 6.

WRITING A NONFICTION BOOK
How to prepare your work for publication

Norman Toulson

'At least you don't have to dream up a plot.' No, but you need to seize and hold your readers' attention as firmly as the author of a whodunnit. In this book Norman Toulson guides the would-be author along the road from ambition to publication. He describes how to collect facts and figures, and plan your information in chapters. He tells you how to find a publisher and sell your concept of the book to him. He shows how you can breathe life into your draft and polish it until it shines. He adds how you can co-operate with the publisher to turn your manuscript into a book and sell it to the public. Norman Toulson has had seven non-fiction books published. They deal with various topics. One evoked the comment, 'I never knew the history of an insurance company could be so enthralling.'

160pp. illus. 1 85703 426 0.

How To Books provide practical help on a large range of topics. They are available through all good bookshops or can be ordered direct from the distributors. Just tick the titles you want and complete the form on the following page.

___ Apply to an Industrial Tribunal (£7.99)
___ Applying for a Job (£7.99)
___ Applying for a United States Visa (£15.99)
___ Be a Freelance Journalist (£8.99)
___ Be a Freelance Secretary (£8.99)
___ Be a Local Councillor (£8.99)
___ Be an Effective School Governor (£9.99)
___ Become a Freelance Sales Agent (£9.99)
___ Become an Au Pair (£8.99)
___ Buy & Run a Shop (£8.99)
___ Buy & Run a Small Hotel (£8.99)
___ Cash from your Computer (£9.99)
___ Career Planning for Women (£8.99)
___ Choosing a Nursing Home (£8.99)
___ Claim State Benefits (£9.99)
___ Communicate at Work (£7.99)
___ Conduct Staff Appraisals (£7.99)
___ Conducting Effective Interviews (£8.99)
___ Copyright & Law for Writers (£8.99)
___ Counsel People at Work (£7.99)
___ Creating a Twist in the Tale (£8.99)
___ Creative Writing (£9.99)
___ Critical Thinking for Students (£8.99)
___ Do Voluntary Work Abroad (£8.99)
___ Do Your Own Advertising (£8.99)
___ Do Your Own PR (£8.99)
___ Doing Business Abroad (£9.99)
___ Emigrate (£9.99)
___ Employ & Manage Staff (£8.99)
___ Find Temporary Work Abroad (£8.99)
___ Finding a Job in Canada (£9.99)
___ Finding a Job in Computers (£8.99)
___ Finding a Job in New Zealand (£9.99)
___ Finding a Job with a Future (£8.99)
___ Finding Work Overseas (£9.99)
___ Freelance DJ-ing (£8.99)
___ Get a Job Abroad (£10.99)
___ Get a Job in America (£9.99)
___ Get a Job in Australia (£9.99)
___ Get a Job in Europe (£9.99)
___ Get a Job in France (£9.99)
___ Get a Job in Germany (£9.99)
___ Get a Job in Hotels and Catering (£8.99)
___ Get a Job in Travel & Tourism (£8.99)
___ Get into Films & TV (£8.99)
___ Get into Radio (£8.99)
___ Get That Job (£6.99)
___ Getting your First Job (£8.99)
___ Going to University (£8.99)
___ Helping your Child to Read (£8.99)
___ Investing in People (£8.99)
___ Invest in Stocks & Shares (£8.99)

___ Keep Business Accounts (£7.99)
___ Know Your Rights at Work (£8.99)
___ Know Your Rights: Teachers (£6.99)
___ Live & Work in America (£9.99)
___ Live & Work in Australia (£12.99)
___ Live & Work in Germany (£9.99)
___ Live & Work in Greece (£9.99)
___ Live & Work in Italy (£8.99)
___ Live & Work in New Zealand (£9.99)
___ Live & Work in Portugal (£9.99)
___ Live & Work in Spain (£7.99)
___ Live & Work in the Gulf (£9.99)
___ Living & Working in Britain (£8.99)
___ Living & Working in China (£9.99)
___ Living & Working in Hong Kong (£10.99)
___ Living & Working in Israel (£10.99)
___ Living & Working in Japan (£8.99)
___ Living & Working in Saudi Arabia (£12.99)
___ Living & Working in the Netherlands (£9.99)
___ Lose Weight & Keep Fit (£6.99)
___ Make a Wedding Speech (£7.99)
___ Making a Complaint (£8.99)
___ Manage a Sales Team (£8.99)
___ Manage an Office (£8.99)
___ Manage Computers at Work (£8.99)
___ Manage People at Work (£8.99)
___ Manage Your Career (£8.99)
___ Managing Budgets & Cash Flows (£9.99)
___ Managing Meetings (£8.99)
___ Managing Your Personal Finances (£8.99)
___ Market Yourself (£8.99)
___ Master Book-Keeping (£8.99)
___ Mastering Business English (£8.99)
___ Master GCSE Accounts (£8.99)
___ Master Languages (£8.99)
___ Master Public Speaking (£8.99)
___ Obtaining Visas & Work Permits (£9.99)
___ Organising Effective Training (£9.99)
___ Pass Exams Without Anxiety (£7.99)
___ Pass That Interview (£6.99)
___ Plan a Wedding (£7.99)
___ Prepare a Business Plan (£8.99)
___ Publish a Book (£9.99)
___ Publish a Newsletter (£9.99)
___ Raise Funds & Sponsorship (£7.99)
___ Rent & Buy Property in France (£9.99)
___ Rent & Buy Property in Italy (£9.99)
___ Retire Abroad (£8.99)
___ Return to Work (£7.99)
___ Run a Local Campaign (£6.99)
___ Run a Voluntary Group (£8.99)
___ Sell Your Business (£9.99)

To: Plymbridge Distributors Ltd, Plymbridge House, Estover Road, Plymouth PL6 7PZ. Customer Services Tel: (01752) 202301. Fax: (01752) 202331.

Please send me copies of the titles I have indicated. Please add postage & packing (UK £1, Europe including Eire, £2, World £3 airmail).

☐ I enclose cheque/PO payable to Plymbridge Distributors Ltd for £ _____

☐ Please charge to my ☐ MasterCard, ☐ Visa, ☐ AMEX card.

Account No. ☐☐☐☐☐☐☐☐☐☐☐☐☐☐

Card Expiry Date ☐ ☐ 19 ☎ **Credit Card orders may be faxed or phoned.**

Customer Name (CAPITALS) ....

Address ....

.... Postcode ....

Telephone .... Signature ....

Every effort will be made to despatch your copy as soon as possible but to avoid possible disappointment please allow up to 21 days for despatch time (42 days if overseas). Prices and availability are subject to change without notice.

Code BPA